D1546775

ALLIED CARRIER AIRCRAFT OF WORLD WAR II

ALLIED CARRIER AIRCRAFT OF WORLD WAR II
1939–1945

EDWARD WARD

First published in 2022

Copyright © 2022 Amber Books Ltd

Published by Amber Books Ltd
United House
London N7 9DP
United Kingdom
www.amberbooks.co.uk
Facebook: amberbooks
Instagram: amberbooksltd
Twitter: @amberbooks
Pinterest: amberbooksltd

ISBN: 978-1-83886-210-7

Editor: Michael Spilling
Designer: Andrew Easton
Picture research: Terry Forshaw

Printed in Slovenia

Contents

Introduction

Naval aviation came of age in World War II. Though tentative early missions had occurred during World War I, culminating in the first ever carrier strike in July 1918, these were restricted by the limited capability of contemporary aircraft.

The inter-war period saw gradual improvement in both the ships and the aircraft carried aboard them. The obvious potential of the aircraft to strike at enemy vessels beyond the range of the most powerful battleship's guns was not lost on naval planners. Even before the war the aircraft carrier was beginning to be viewed as the most important ship in the fleet in both the US and Royal Navies.

On the outbreak of war in September 1939, the Royal Navy possessed seven aircraft carriers and the United States five, though the latter nation would bring two more into service by the time of the Pearl Harbor attack of December 1941. Neither Navy had as many carriers as they wanted due to the terms of the 1922 Washington Treaty which restricted the total tonnage that could be used for each class of ship. The outbreak of war saw this treaty abandoned and Britain would commission into service a further 76 carriers of all types by VJ Day. It should be mentioned that France also possessed a carrier, *Béarn,* but this vessel was never used to conduct operational flying, so for the first two

The British Blackburn Roc included four 7.7mm (0.303in) Browning machine guns in a power-operated dorsal turret.

years of war Allied carrier operations were exclusively conducted by the British, with somewhat mixed results. Whilst major milestones were achieved such as sinking the first capital ship by aircraft during wartime and critically contributing to the destruction of the *Bismarck,* British carrier aircraft had proven inferior to shore-based fighters and the fleet carriers *Courageous*, *Glorious* and *Ark Royal* had all been lost before December 1941.

Carrier power

When the Japanese attacked Pearl Harbor, in the world's first coordinated large scale carrier strike, no US carriers were lost because all were at sea, a fact that would prove critical in the months that followed. Meanwhile the awesome industrial capability of the United States saw an incredible 151 aircraft carriers launched during the war, 122 of which were smaller escort carriers, many of which were supplied to the UK. In May 1942, the Battle of the Coral Sea saw the first engagement in history during which the surface vessels of both

navies never came within visual range of each other and all the offensive action was conducted by aircraft. The battles of the Pacific war remain the only large engagements by two sides both possessing aircraft carriers and saw the gradual attrition of the Japanese naval air arm such that it was effectively removed as a meaningful opponent. Meanwhile, in the West, US and British fleet carriers supported the invasions of Africa and Italy whilst both nations operated small escort carriers to protect the vital convoys steaming across the Atlantic from U-boat and aerial attack.

Catapult launched planes

It should be remembered that not all shipborne aircraft flew from carriers during the war. Many of the world's capital ships carried a floatplane or small flying boat for gunnery spotting (vital in the early pre-radar naval battles), reconnaissance, air sea rescue and other tasks, these being launched by catapult and recovered by crane after alighting on the water.

Primarily used by the US Navy in the Pacific theatre, the Curtiss SB2C Helldiver had become the main dive-bomber and attack aircraft of USN carriers by the end of the war.

FIGHTERS

Allied carrier fighters followed two distinct paths in the lead up to World War II. The British favoured a two-seater approach with a dedicated navigator, but the US built single-seat fighters, conceptually similar to their land-based counterparts. The latter approach proved to be the correct one, as the Royal Navy adapted RAF single-seat fighters to their needs, with mixed results, and took delivery of as many American fighters as possible.

This chapter includes the following aircraft:

- Grumman Goblin I
- Gloster Sea Gladiator
- Grumman F4F Wildcat
- Brewster F2A Buffalo
- Blackburn Roc
- Fairey Fulmar
- Vought F4U Corsair
- Hawker Sea Hurricane
- Fairey Firefly
- Supermarine Seafire
- Blackburn Firebrand
- Grumman F6F Hellcat
- Grumman F7F Tigercat
- Ryan FR-1 Fireball
- Grumman F8F Bearcat
- McDonnell FH-1 Phantom
- Hawker Sea Fury
- de Havilland Sea Hornet

The preeminent Allied naval fighter until the introduction of the Hellcat onto carrier decks in 1943, the pugnacious Grumman Wildcat proved crucial in halting Japanese expansion in the Pacific. These General Motors-built FM-1s were flying out of NAS Cherry Point, California, in 1943.

Grumman Goblin I

Grumman's first aircraft design, the FF, set a precedent for the company's future products by combining immense structural strength with technological innovation to produce a thoroughly effective aircraft.

Before they made complete aircraft, Grumman supplied components to other manufacturers and the US Navy's request that they supply a retractable undercarriage unit for use on Boeing F4B-1 fighters prompted the company to propose a completely new fighter design instead. The prototype of the new XFF-1 two seat fighter was the first world's first carrier aircraft with retractable undercarriage, and when fitted with its definitive Wright Cyclone engine clocked 323km/h (201mph), which was faster than any fighter then in US Navy service. Production aircraft began serving with VF-5B on USS *Lexington* in June 1933 and the aircraft remained in frontline US service until late 1940.

Spanish Civil War service

By this time the FF had seen service in the Spanish Civil War, in the process scoring the only recorded air-to-air victory by a Grumman biplane design by shooting down a Heinkel He 51,

Grumman SF-1

The SF-1 was a variant of Grumman's two-seat biplane optimized for scouting duties. This example was serving with VS-3B aboard USS *Lexington* in 1935.

though the Spanish Grummans, referred to by Republican forces as the G.23 Delfin (Dolphin) were actually licence-built examples constructed by the Canadian Car & Foundry Company. The RCAF had initially rejected the aircraft due to its slow speed but the with outbreak of war, 15 were taken on strength and named the Goblin I. Serving with 118 Squadron RCAF between September 1940 and April 1942, the Goblins flew from Dartmouth, Nova Scotia, on anti-submarine patrols and maritime reconnaissance. Shockingly, given their manifest obsolescence by this time, the 15 Grumman Goblins represented the sole fighter presence on the east coast of Canada until they were supplemented by Curtiss Kittyhawks late in 1941.

Grumman Goblin I

Weight: (Maximum take-off) 2256kg (4973lb)

Dimensions: Length: 8m (24ft 10in), Wingspan: 10.6m (34ft 6in), Height: 2.9m (9ft 6in)

Powerplant: One 597kW (800hp) Wright R-1820-F52 Cyclone nine-cylinder air-cooled radial engine

Speed: 560km/h (216mph)

Range: 1,014 km (630 miles)

Ceiling: 7255m (23,800ft)

Crew: 2

Armament: Two fixed forward firing 7.62mm (0.3in) Browning machine guns and two flexibly mounted 7.62mm (0.3in) Browning machine guns in rear cockpit

Gloster Sea Gladiator

The only carrier-based fighter biplane to see combat during World War II, the Sea Gladiator's career was brief but intense and it would secure enduring fame for its role in the defence of Malta.

The Gloster Gladiator, the last British biplane fighter to be produced, was a more powerful and aerodynamically improved development of Gloster's Gauntlet and had first flown in September 1934. Obsolescent even as it entered RAF service in early 1937, its frontline service with Fighter Command in the UK was relatively brief as more capable monoplane fighters entered service. As a result, when the Air Ministry was looking at potential RAF designs to convert for carrier use the Gladiator appeared an ideal candidate for a readily available stop-gap conversion pending the arrival of the more advanced Fairey Fulmar, itself originally an RAF project.

Sea Gladiator (interim)

The first 38 Mk.II Gladiators were therefore transferred to the FAA and converted for carrier operations. The fuselage structure was strengthened, an arrestor hook fitted and some

Gloster Sea Gladiator Mk.II
Pictured as it appeared when serving with 813 Squadron aboard HMS *Eagle* during operations in the Mediterranean during 1940, this Sea Gladiator Mk.II wears the standard FAA colours of Extra Dark Sea Grey and Dark Slate Grey over Sky Grey.

changes were made to the internal equipment, for example a Naval TR9 radio was fitted and the airspeed indicator was calibrated in knots rather than mph. In this form the aircraft were known as the Sea Gladiator (interim) and were delivered to the Fleet Air Arm in December 1938. By this time the Admiralty had ordered 60 examples of a more comprehensively navalized aircraft, the Sea Gladiator Mk.II fitted with spools for catapult launching and dinghy stowage between the gear legs. These aircraft were not conversions but built by Gloster from scratch as naval aircraft.

Following successful carrier trials with 801 squadron, during the course

Gloster Sea Gladiator Mk.II
Weight: (Maximum takeoff) 2277kg (5019lb)
Dimensions: Length: 8.36m (27ft 5in), Wingspan: 9.83m (32ft 3in), Height: 3.58m (11ft 9in)
Powerplant: One 630kW (840hp) Bristol Mercury VIIIAS 9-cylinder air-cooled radial piston engine
Speed: 407km/h (253mph)
Range: 670km (415 miles)
Ceiling: 10,210m (33,500ft)
Crew: 1
Armament: Two 7.62mm (0.303in) Browning machine guns fixed forward-firing in forward fuselage, two 7.62mm (0.303in) Browning machine guns fixed forward-firing under wings

of which over 200 arrested landings were undertaken during February 1939, the Sea Gladiators went to sea with 802 Squadron aboard HMS *Glorious*. On the outbreak of war *Glorious*, with nine Sea Gladiators aboard, was sent to protect merchant shipping in the Indian Ocean but was soon recalled to join the Norwegian campaign. Called upon to transport the standard Gloster Gladiators of 263 Squadron RAF to Norway, FAA pilots landed the non-navalized Gladiators on the carrier despite these aircraft possessing no arrestor hook. In Norwegian waters the Sea Gladiator scored its first victories, a Ju 87 Stuka and Heinkel He 111 falling to Sea Gladiators of 802 Squadron. Further victories followed throughout 1939 and 40 for Sea Gladiators operating in defence of the major Royal Navy port at Scapa Flow, in the Orkney Islands, and in skirmishes over the Mediterranean aboard HMS *Illustrious* and HMS *Eagle*.

Regia Aeronautica

The Sea Gladiator's enduring claim to fame, however, derived from its use in Malta. Sea Gladiators in crates were held in Malta to supply replacements when necessary to the carriers of the Mediterranean fleet. During the spring of 1940, increased Italian air activity spurred the formation of the RAF station fighter flight at Hal Far airfield equipped with hastily uncrated Sea Gladiators.

Subsequently, when Italy declared war on the UK and France on 10 June 1940, the entire fighter force of Malta facing the might of the *Regia Aeronautica* consisted of six Sea Gladiators. Flown by RAF pilots, the dinghy pack and arrestor hook were removed to save weight and three-bladed variable pitch propellers fitted. One airframe received the entire engine and cowling from a Bristol Blenheim in an attempt to improve performance, which was dubbed the 'Bleriator'.

Over the course of the year the Sea Gladiators were plunged into intense action. Latterly supplemented by Hawker Hurricanes, the last survivor of the Maltese Sea Gladiators flew its final mission, a meteorological reconnaissance, in January 1942.

Gloster Sea Gladiator Mk.II

Resplendent in its silver pre-war colour scheme, N2219 of 802 squadron displays the broad yellow fuselage chevron denoting that the aircraft is operating from the carrier HMS *Glorious*.

Grumman F4F Wildcat

The most important Allied naval fighter of the first half of the war, the Wildcat was not particularly fast but was well armed, manoeuvrable, easy to operate from a carrier and possessed exceptional strength.

When the US Navy issued a specification for a new shipboard fighter in 1935, Grumman proposed a smaller and more powerful development of its successful F3F biplane fighter to be designated the F4F-1. However, the appearance of the Brewster F2A monoplane, designed to the same specification as the biplane F4F but offering a much greater predicted capability, prompted second thoughts at both Grumman and the Navy on the future of the F4F. Grumman responded by proposing a completely new monoplane design in place of the biplane F4F-1 that met with immediate acceptance by the Navy. The prototype XF4F-1 was cancelled and a new contract placed with Grumman for the monoplane XF4F-2 in July 1936.

Despite starting their design process somewhat later than Brewster, Grumman managed to complete the XF4F-2 before the rival XF2A-1 and the first flight was made by Robert L. Hall on 2 September 1937. The XF4F-2

suffered developmental problems, including a forced landing due to engine failure in April 1938 that may have hastened the Navy's decision in June to select the Brewster F2A as its first monoplane fighter over the Grumman machine. Convinced that the F4F was a design of considerable potential, Grumman proposed utilizing a more powerful version of the Pratt and Whitney Twin Wasp with a two-speed, two-stage supercharger allowing the engine to maintain maximum power output at a greater altitude.

Redesign

The new engine was considerably heavier than the unit it replaced, necessitating a redesign of wings of greater span and area. The redesign also resulted in the elegantly curved surfaces of both wing and tail being replaced by an angular planform that was to become something of a trademark of Grumman design for years to come. The prototype was

Grumman F4F-3

Weight: (Maximum takeoff) 3367kg (7423lb)
Dimensions: Length: 8.76m (28ft 9in), Wingspan: 11.59m (38ft), Height: 3.61m (11ft 10in)
Powerplant: One 895kW (1200hp) Pratt & Whitney R-1830-86 Twin Wasp 14-cylinder air-cooled radial piston engine
Speed: 515km/h (320mph)
Range: 1360km (845 miles)
Ceiling: 12,000m (39,500ft)
Crew: 1
Armament: Six 12.7mm (0.5in) AN/M2 Browning machine guns fixed forward-firing in wings; up to 90kg (200lb) bombload under wings

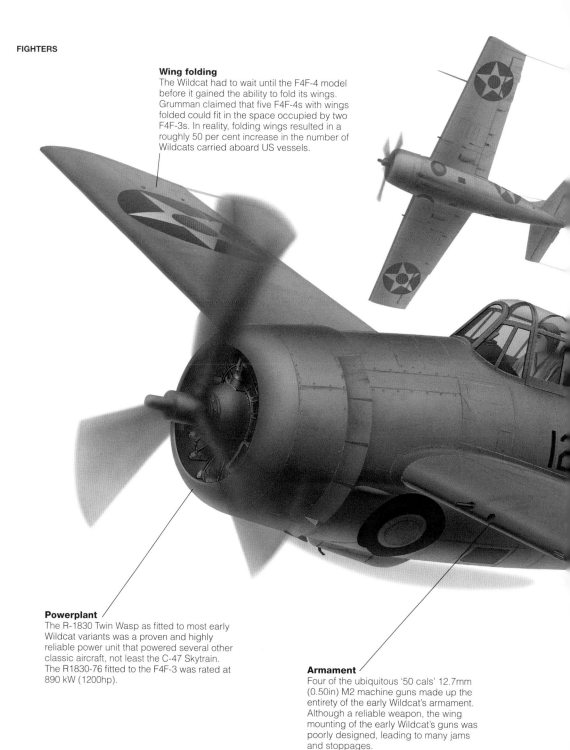

Wing folding
The Wildcat had to wait until the F4F-4 model before it gained the ability to fold its wings. Grumman claimed that five F4F-4s with wings folded could fit in the space occupied by two F4F-3s. In reality, folding wings resulted in a roughly 50 per cent increase in the number of Wildcats carried aboard US vessels.

Powerplant
The R-1830 Twin Wasp as fitted to most early Wildcat variants was a proven and highly reliable power unit that powered several other classic aircraft, not least the C-47 Skytrain. The R1830-76 fitted to the F4F-3 was rated at 890 kW (1200hp).

Armament
Four of the ubiquitous '50 cals' 12.7mm (0.50in) M2 machine guns made up the entirety of the early Wildcat's armament. Although a reliable weapon, the wing mounting of the early Wildcat's guns was poorly designed, leading to many jams and stoppages.

Grumman F4F-3, Tafuna, Samoa, 1941

These F4F-3s of VMF-121 are shown as they appeared at America's introduction to the war in December 1941. The red dots in the national markings were soon discarded to preclude any possible confusion with the Japanese *hinomaru* marking. Re-equipped with the F4F-4, VMF-121 formed a part of the 'Cactus Air Force' that formed the Allied air component during the Guadalcanal campaign of 1942 and 1943.

Grumman F4F-3

Weight: (Maximum takeoff) 3367kg (7423lb)

Dimensions: Length: 8.76m (28ft 9in), Wingspan: 11.59m (38ft), Height: 3.61m (11ft 10in)

Powerplant: One 895kW (1200hp) Pratt & Whitney R-1830-86 Twin Wasp 14-cylinder air-cooled radial piston engine

Speed: 515km/h (320mph)

Range: 1360km (845 miles)

Ceiling: 12,000m (39,500ft)

Crew: 1

Armament: Six 12.7mm (0.5in) AN/M2 Browning machine guns fixed forward-firing in wings; up to 90kg (200lb) bombload under wings

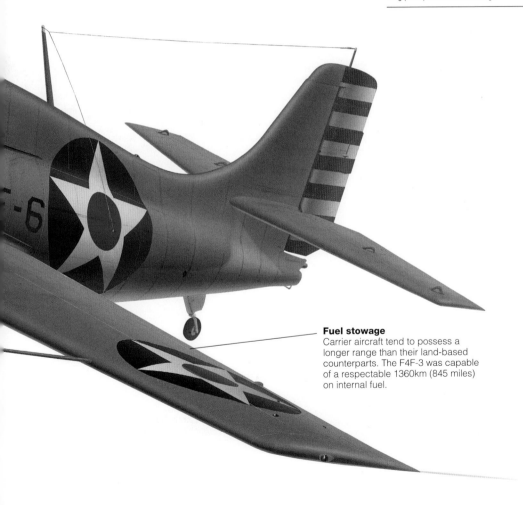

Fuel stowage
Carrier aircraft tend to possess a longer range than their land-based counterparts. The F4F-3 was capable of a respectable 1360km (845 miles) on internal fuel.

Grumman F4F-4

Another Marine Corps Wildcat Medal of Honor recipient, Joe Foss shot down all 26 of his confirmed victories during a three month period over Guadalcanal to become the ranking Marine Corps 'ace' during 1942. Foss flew this F4F-4 during October of that year.

Eastern Aircraft FM-2

The FM-2, built exclusively by General Motors Eastern Aircraft Division, was produced in greater numbers than any other single Wildcat variant. This example was serving with VC-4 aboard the escort carrier USS *White Plains* during the battle of Leyte Gulf in October 1944.

rebuilt and flew for the first time in its new form as the XF4F-3 on 12 February 1939 and immediately demonstrated a performance superior to both its progenitor and the Brewster F2A. Further test flying to eliminate handling issues took place into 1940 and resulted in numerous changes, the most significant being an increase to the dihedral of the wings and the repositioning of the horizontal tail surfaces from the rear fuselage to the tail fin. Grumman received a contract for the first batch of F4F-3s in August 1939 and the first production took to the air in February 1940, the second following in July, both these aircraft subsequently being used for intensive

Grumman F4F-4

Weight: (Maximum takeoff) 3978kg (8762lb)
Dimensions: Length: 8.85m (29ft), Wingspan: 11.59m (38ft), Height: 3.44m (11ft 4in)
Powerplant: One 895kW (1200hp) Pratt & Whitney R-1830-86 Twin Wasp 14-cylinder air-cooled radial piston engine
Speed: 515km/h (320mph)
Range: 2051km (1275 miles) with external tanks
Ceiling: 10370m (34,000ft)
Crew: 1
Armament: Six 12.7mm (0.5in) AN/M2 Browning machine guns fixed forward-firing in wings; up to 90kg (200lb) bombload under wings

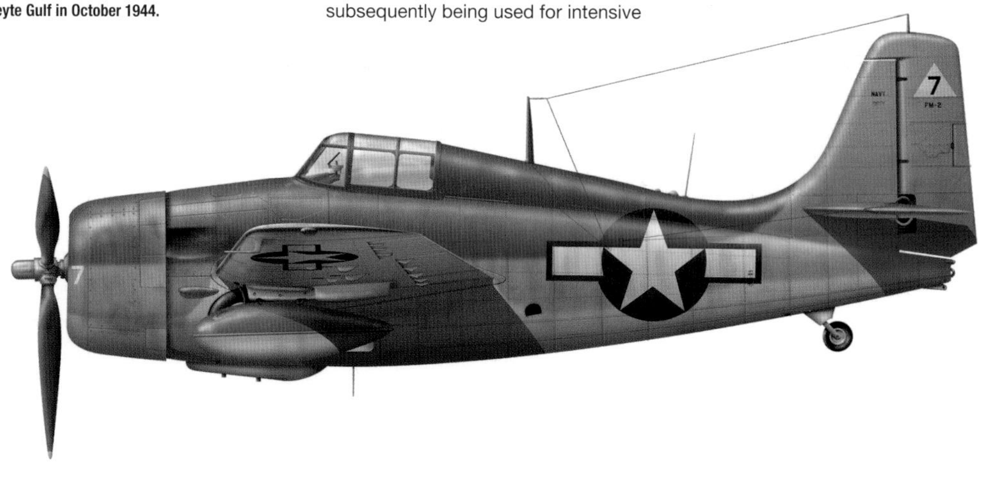

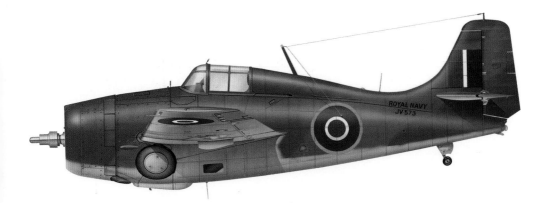

development flying. In October the US Navy adopted the name 'Wildcat' for the F4F, thus initiating an unbroken line of US Navy Grumman 'cats' that would only end when the F-14 Tomcat was retired in 2006.

European orders

The aircraft had already elicited considerable foreign interest and orders were placed by both France and the UK during 1940. The French Aéronavale aircraft were to be powered by the Wright R-1820 Cyclone as the G-36A, fitted with French Darne 7.5mm (0.3in) machine guns, and feature French radios and gunsights. In the event France fell before the aircraft could be delivered and the order was taken up by the UK as the Martlet I, becoming the first F4Fs to enter operational service anywhere when deliveries began in July 1940. Two of these aircraft became the first US-built aircraft in British service to claim a combat victory when they shot down a Junkers Ju 88 over the Orkney Islands on Christmas Day 1940. Subsequent British aircraft were powered by the 895kw (1200hp) Pratt & Whitney S3C4-G with a two-speed supercharger and folding wings, although to expedite deliveries the

Royal Navy agreed to take the first 10 of the order for 100 without the folding wing capability, these aircraft being named the Martlet II.

Meanwhile, deliveries of production aircraft to the US Navy began in December 1940 with the first examples being used to equip VF-7 and VF-4 aboard USS *Wasp* and USS *Ranger* respectively in January 1941. Early aircraft suffered from a propensity for the wing-mounted flotation bags to inflate of their own accord, throwing the aircraft into an uncontrollable dive. The US Navy discarded the bags but not before at least one fatal accident occurred due to such a failure and they remained a feature of export F4Fs.

Another feature that was disliked by pilots, although not actually dangerous, was the manually-retracted undercarriage, requiring around 30 turns of a handle to raise and lower. Although this was a common feature on contemporary aircraft, such as early Spitfires, the F4F was never to be fitted with a powered retraction system. In general the introduction of the F4F to service had proved relatively smooth and further contracts were placed with Grumman for the F4F-3 and F4F-3A that featured the more powerful engine as fitted to the RN's Martlet IIs.

Grumman Wildcat Mk.V

Flying off escort carrier HMS *Vindex* in early 1945, Sub Lt R.A. Fleischmann Allen used this General Motors built Wildcat V (equivalent to the US FM-1) to shoot down a Junkers Ju 88 and share in the destruction of an Fw 200 Condor. Unlike the US Navy, the RN referred to all Wildcats as Grummans, regardless of who had manufactured them.

Wildcat Mk.V

Weight: (Maximum takeoff) 3978kg (8762lb)
Dimensions: Length: 8.85m (29ft), Wingspan: 11.59m (38ft), Height: 3.44m (11ft 4in)
Powerplant: One 895kW (1200hp) Pratt & Whitney R-1830-86 Twin Wasp 14-cylinder air-cooled radial piston engine
Speed: 515km/h (320mph)
Range: 2051km (1275 miles) with external tanks
Ceiling: 10,100m (33,200ft)
Crew: 1
Armament: Four 12.7mm (0.5in) AN/M2 Browning machine guns fixed forward-firing in wings; up to 225kg (500lb) bombload under wings

---

When the US entered World War II Navy and Marine squadrons possessed 245 Wildcats and the F4F was plunged into intense action almost immediately in the desperate defence of Wake Island during December 1941, scoring its first combat victories in US service. Remarkably, during this action Captain Henry Elrod managed to sink the

Cutaway key

1 Starboard navigation light
2 Wingtip
3 Starboard formation light
4 Rear spar
5 Aileron construction
6 Fixed aileron tab
7 All riveted wing construction
8 Lateral stiffeners
9 Forward canted main spar
10 'Crimped' leading-edge ribs
11 Solid web forward ribs
12 Starboard outer gun blast tube
13 Carburettor air duct
14 Intake
15 Curtiss three-bladed, constant speed propeller
16 Propeller cuffs
17 Propeller hub
18 Engine front face
19 Pressure baffle
20 Forward cowling ring
21 Cooler intake
22 Cooler air duct
23 Pratt & Whitney R 1830-86 radial engine
24 Rear cowling ring/flap support
25 Controllable cowling flaps
26 Downdraft ram air duct
27 Engine mounting ring
28 Anti-detonant regulator unit
29 Cartridge starter
30 Generator
31 Intercooler
32 Engine accessories
33 Bearer assembly welded cluster joint
34 Main beam
35 Lower cowl flap
36 Exhaust stub
37 Starboard mainwheel
38 Undercarriage fairing
39 Lower drag link
40 Hydraulic brake
41 Port mainwheel
42 Detachable hub cover
43 Low-pressure tyre
44 Axle forging
45 Upper drag link
46 Oleo shock strut
47 Ventral fairing
48 Wheel well
49 Pivot point
50 Landing light

51 Main forging
52 Compression link
53 Gun camera port
54 Counter balance
55 Anti-detonant tank
56 Retraction sprocket
57 Gear box
58 Stainless steel firewall
59 Engine bearers
60 Actuation chain (undercarriage)
61 Engine oil tank
62 Oil filler
63 Hoisting sling installation
64 Bullet resistant windscreen
65 Reflector gunsight
66 Panoramic rearview mirror
67 Wing fold position

68 Adjustable headrest
69 Shoulder harness
70 Canopy track sill
71 Pilot's adjustable seat
72 Instrument panel shroud
73 Undercarriage manual crank
74 Control column
75 Rudder pedals
76 Fuselage/front spar attachment
77 Main fuel filler cap
78 Seat harness attachment
79 Back armour
80 Oxygen cylinder
81 Reserve fuel filler cap
82 Alternative transmitter/receiver (ABA or IFF) installation
83 Battery
84 IFF and ABA dynamotor units

85 Wing flap vacuum tank
86 Handhold
87 Turnover bar
88 Rearward-sliding plexiglas canopy
89 Streamlined aerial mast
90 Mast support
91 One-man Mk IA life-raft stowage
92 Upper longeron

93 Toolkit
94 Aerial lead-in
95 Elevator and rudder control runs
96 'L'-section fuselage frames
97 IFF aerial
98 Dorsal lights
99 Whip aerial
100 Wing-fold jury strut
101 Fin fairing
102 Access panel
103 Tailwheel strut extension arm
104 Rudder trim tab control flexible shaft
105 Tailplane rib profile
106 Starboard tailplane

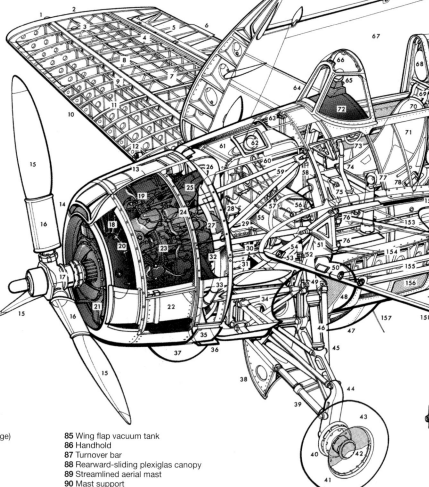

F4F-4 Wildcat

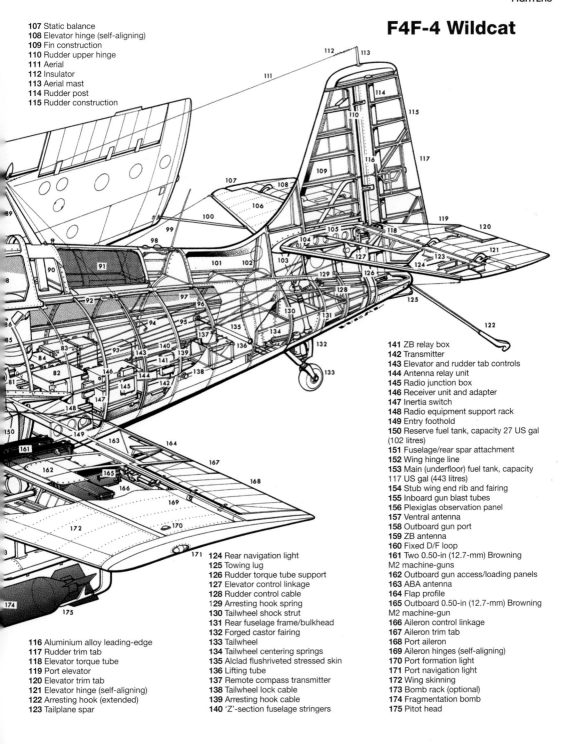

107 Static balance
108 Elevator hinge (self-aligning)
109 Fin construction
110 Rudder upper hinge
111 Aerial
112 Insulator
113 Aerial mast
114 Rudder post
115 Rudder construction

141 ZB relay box
142 Transmitter
143 Elevator and rudder tab controls
144 Antenna relay unit
145 Radio junction box
146 Receiver unit and adapter
147 Inertia switch
148 Radio equipment support rack
149 Entry foothold
150 Reserve fuel tank, capacity 27 US gal (102 litres)
151 Fuselage/rear spar attachment
152 Wing hinge line
153 Main (underfloor) fuel tank, capacity 117 US gal (443 litres)
154 Stub wing end rib and fairing
155 Inboard gun blast tubes
156 Plexiglas observation panel
157 Ventral antenna
158 Outboard gun port
159 ZB antenna
160 Fixed D/F loop
161 Two 0.50-in (12.7-mm) Browning M2 machine-guns
162 Outboard gun access/loading panels
163 ABA antenna
164 Flap profile
165 Outboard 0.50-in (12.7-mm) Browning M2 machine-gun
166 Aileron control linkage
167 Aileron trim tab
168 Port aileron
169 Aileron hinges (self-aligning)
170 Port formation light
171 Port navigation light
172 Wing skinning
173 Bomb rack (optional)
174 Fragmentation bomb
175 Pitot head

116 Aluminium alloy leading-edge
117 Rudder trim tab
118 Elevator torque tube
119 Port elevator
120 Elevator trim tab
121 Elevator hinge (self-aligning)
122 Arresting hook (extended)
123 Tailplane spar

124 Rear navigation light
125 Towing lug
126 Rudder torque tube support
127 Elevator control linkage
128 Rudder control cable
129 Arresting hook spring
130 Tailwheel shock strut
131 Rear fuselage frame/bulkhead
132 Forged castor fairing
133 Tailwheel
134 Tailwheel centering springs
135 Alclad flushriveted stressed skin
136 Lifting tube
137 Remote compass transmitter
138 Tailwheel lock cable
139 Arresting hook cable
140 'Z'-section fuselage stringers

Grumman F4F-4

Marion Carl became the first Marine Corps 'ace' of World War II on 29 August 1942 when he shot down his fifth enemy aircraft over Guadalcanal. He would go on to score a total of 18.5 victories, seeing operational service again during the Vietnam War.

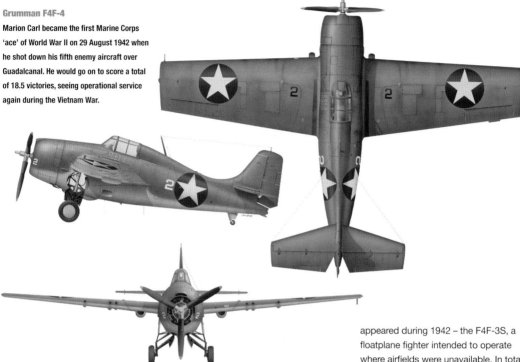

Japanese destroyer *Kisaragi* with the Wildcat's modest bombload.

F4F-4

By this time Grumman's attention had switched to the F4F-4 that, as well as featuring two extra 12.7mm (0.50in) wing guns, introduced the important improvement of folding wings, utilizing Grumman's patented 'sto-wing' system that allowed the wings to swing through 90 degrees and backwards to be stored alongside the fuselage. This feature effectively doubled the number of Wildcats that could be accommodated on any given carrier and sealed its ascendancy over the Brewster F2A, which never featured a folding wing.

The F4F-4 entered service in December 1941, quickly becoming the most numerous variant, and all the USN units committed to the decisive

Battle of Midway in June 1942 were equipped, at least in part, with F4F-4s. These were also supplied to Britain as the Martlet III. By the time of the Guadalcanal campaign a long-range photo-reconnaissance Wildcat had entered service, the F4F-7, of which only 21 were built. The F4F-7 was unarmed, carried a single camera and featured a 2594-litre (685-US gallon) internal fuel capacity sufficient to give it a potential endurance of 24 hours!

F4F-5

During 1942, the F4F-5, a version equipped with the Wright Cyclone engine, was flown for comparative flight tests with the standard Twin Wasp powered version and although a US contract did not materialize, this variant did see service with the Royal Navy as the Martlet IV. Another unusual variant

appeared during 1942 – the F4F-3S, a floatplane fighter intended to operate where airfields were unavailable. In total 100 sets of floats were produced to convert F4F-3s for maritime operations, but apart from the prototype none were ever used.

During the same year General Motors began production of the F4F-4, although with only four wing guns, as the FM-1 (or Martlet V in the UK) eventually producing 1600 examples. By 1943, with Grumman concentrating on Hellcat development and production, General Motors undertook total responsibility for Wildcat production and delivered over 4400 (over half of total Wildcat production) of the F4F-8, the final version being instantly recognizable due to its taller vertical tail. Primarily used on escort carriers, too small to handle larger, more modern fighters, this final Wildcat was supplied to both the US as the FM-2 and UK as the Wildcat VI, the Martlet name having been dropped in March 1944.

Brewster F2A Buffalo

The US Navy's first monoplane fighter delivered a significant upgrade in performance over the biplanes that preceded it. Unfortunately, the F2A failed to live up to its initial promise.

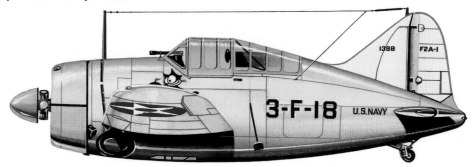

Brewster, a coachbuilding company founded in 1810, were relatively new to the aviation scene when they won a contract to supply the US Navy with its first modern cantilever monoplane fighter. The US Navy had long held the opinion that the landing speed of the monoplane was too great for carrier operations, but as the biplane reached the end of its development potential it was decided to give the monoplane a chance and accordingly the prototype Brewster XF2A-1 was ordered along with Grumman's biplane XF4F-1 as a back-up.

The XF2A-1 that emerged in early 1938 was a distinctly rotund but pugnacious aircraft. Although it could hardly be called sleek it possessed such advanced features as a fully flush riveted stressed skin construction, split flaps and hydraulically powered retractable undercarriage, a far cry from the contemporary hand-cranked undercarriage of Grumman fighters. Making its maiden flight on 2 December 1937, the Brewster was soon found to possess a disappointing top speed of 447km/h (277mph), well below the expected figure.

Brewster F2A-1

This F2A-1 of VF-3 was assigned to USS *Saratoga* in 1939, the first US unit to operate a monoplane fighter at sea. Note the 'Felix the Cat' insignia on the forward fuselage, partially obscured by the wing.

As a result, the XF2A-1 was subjected to trials in NACA's Langley Aeronautical laboratory wind tunnel, becoming the first full-size US aircraft to be so tested, resulting in detail improvements to the fuselage and engine cowling that raised the maximum speed by nearly 50km/h (32mph). Accepted for production as the F2A-1, 54 of this initial model were ordered and delivery of the first examples began in July 1939, but no units had formed on the type by the outbreak of war in Europe. Eleven F2A-1s would be issued to VF-3 on USS *Saratoga* by the end of the year thus becoming the first operational monoplane carrier fighter unit in the US Navy.

Carrier service

The F2A-1 was faster and handled better than early Grumman F4Fs and its initial carrier service was to prove relatively trouble-free. By this time the

Brewster F2A-1

Weight: (Maximum takeoff) 3247kg (7159lb)
Dimensions: Length: 7.92m (26ft 0in), Wingspan: 10.67m (35ft), Height: 3.56m (11ft 8in)
Powerplant: One 700kW (940hp) Wright R-1820-34 Cyclone nine-cylinder air-cooled radial engine
Speed: 501km/h (311mph)
Range: 2486km (1545 miles)
Ceiling: 10,100m (33,200ft)
Crew: 1
Armament: Two 12.7mm (0.5in) M2 Browning machine guns fixed forward firing in wings, one 12.7mm (0.5in) M2 Browning machine gun and one 7.7mm (0.3in) .30 AN/M2 Browning fixed forward firing in cowling

original prototype had been severely damaged in deck-landing trials and the opportunity was taken to re-engine it as the prototype of the faster and more powerful XF2A-2 with the heavier armament of four 12.7mm (0.5in) machine guns, more fuel and other equipment, and 43 examples of this new model were ordered. With the F2A-2 on order the decision was taken to release the balance of the F2A-1 order for export to Finland designated the B-239, the first of many export orders. Belgium and the United Kingdom

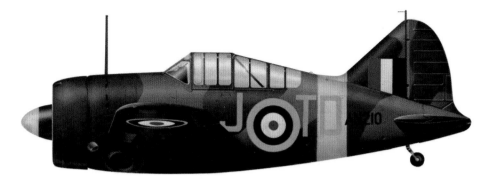

ordered the F2A-2 (known as the B-339 for export) during 1940, although the UK would take over the Belgian aircraft after Belgium fell to the Germans, with the Netherlands East Indies ordering B-339s shortly after. It was the British who bestowed the name 'Buffalo' on the fighter, which swiftly became a popular nickname for the aircraft.

Although the F2A-2 was faster than the F2A-1, the increased weight had not been matched by engine power and performance in all other areas suffered, particularly manoeuvrability. Worse was to come with the development of the F2A-3, of which 108 were ordered

Brewster F2A-2

The second unit to operate the F2A was VF-2, the 'Flying Chiefs', who took their F2A-2s aboard USS *Lexington* for a training cruise to Pearl Harbor in March 1941.

by the US Navy in January 1941. The F2A-3 saw yet more weight added to the airframe, mostly to lengthen the fuselage to fit in a larger fuel tank, but utilized the same engine as the F2A-2 and as a result performance, which was by now hardly sparkling by contemporary standards, was lowered on every count. The increased weight also proved too much for the Buffalo's landing gear and undercarriage failures were relatively commonplace in carrier operations, this being the primary reason for the withdrawal of the F2A from carrier decks. F2As were still aboard *Saratoga* when war was declared but all had been transferred to shore-based roles within a month.

F2A-3

By the time the F2A-3 appeared, earlier variants of the Brewster had seen

Brewster Buffalo Mk.I

Serving with 453 squadron of the Royal Australian Air Force, AN210 was based at Sembawang, Singapore, in November 1941. Buffaloes of this unit were stripped of equipment to save around 450kg (1000lb) of weight and improve performance.

combat, initially with Finland against the Soviet Union. The Finns were fortunate enough to have received the early B-239 before weight gain had taken its unfortunate toll on performance and the Brewster was both highly successful and extremely popular with pilots, achieving an unprecedented victory-to-loss ratio of 32 to one. The B-239 formed the backbone of the Finnish fighter arm until the introduction of the Messerschmitt Bf 109G-2 in mid-1943 and the affection with which it was held can be judged by its nicknames of 'Sky Pearl' and the somewhat inexplicable 'Bustling Walter'.

Brewster F2A-3

Weight: (Maximum takeoff) 3247kg (7159lb)
Dimensions: Length: 8.03m (26ft 4in), Wingspan: 10.67m (35ft), Height: 3.66m (12ft)
Powerplant: One 890kW (1200hp) Wright R-1820-40 Cyclone nine-cylinder air-cooled radial engine
Speed: 517km/h (321mph)
Range: 1553km (965 miles)
Ceiling: 10,100m (33,200ft)
Crew: 1
Armament: Two 12.7mm (0.5in) M2 Browning machine guns fixed forward firing in wings, two 12.7mm (0.5in) M2 Browning machine guns

Finland was also the last nation to fly the Brewster, its final victories being scored on 3 October 1944 when two Junkers Ju 87 Stukas were shot down during the Lapland war against Germany.

Experience with the British and NEI was not so happy. RAF tests saw the Brewster rejected for use in Europe and

Brewster B-239

Ironically, the Brewster F2A achieved its greatest success flying for Finland, a nation that possessed no aircraft carriers and which was fighting against the Allies. Sergeant Heimo Lampi shot down 5.5 aircraft, of his 8.5 total, with various Brewster B-239s, including this one, BW-354, which he flew during September 1942.

nearly all were sent to the Far East where they were expected to be superior to any fighter Japan was likely to field in the event of war. In reality Japanese forces outnumbered the Allies, they possessed superior fighter types and boasted highly experienced aircrew. As a result, virtually all of the British Commonwealth and NEI Brewsters were destroyed by March 1942, although in the process they did inflict substantial losses on the advancing Japanese, four Allied pilots becoming 'aces' on the type.

Oddly, the final nation to take the Brewster into combat was its country of origin, which was also to achieve the worst results with it. The F2A's only major engagement in American hands took place during the Battle of Midway when Marine Corps unit VMF-221 lost 13 out of 20 F2As, mainly due to poor tactics. All Buffaloes remaining in US service were subsequently relegated to the advanced fighter training role, a task at which they excelled, being pleasant and easy to fly and possessing fairly high performance.

Brewster F2A-3

VMF-221 took the F2A into action with American forces for the first and only time on 4 June 1942 at Midway. Losses were catastrophic, only three of the 20 F2As that took off to intercept Japanese bombers were serviceable by 6 June.

Blackburn Roc

Representing a flawed concept applied to an inadequate airframe, the Blackburn Roc was arguably the worst carrier fighter to see combat service during World War II.

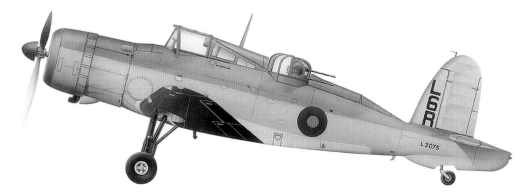

The Air Ministry issued specification O.30/35 for a naval turret fighter at the end of 1935, intended to complement conventionally-armed fighter aircraft. Boulton Paul proposed a navalized Defiant but a turret-equipped variant of Blackburn's Skua was judged superior and 136 examples of the new Blackburn Roc were ordered off the drawing board in July 1937. The Skua was to prove an excellent dive bomber but was far less successful in the air-to-air combat role, so the wisdom of producing a pure fighter development of that aircraft armed solely with a four-gun turret was, at best, questionable. The Air Ministry seems to have had second thoughts too as 127 examples of the Fairey Fulmar were ordered in 1938 as an insurance should the Roc proved a failure, a decision that would ultimately prove extremely fortuitous.

Reduced fuel capacity

Blackburn were at full capacity building the Skua and Botha so production of the Roc was contracted to Boulton Paul, who by this time had already flown the prototype Defiant, a turret fighter nearly a third faster than the lumbering Roc. The first Roc flew on Christmas Eve 1938, and while pleasant to fly it could barely exceed 322km/h (200mph) and endurance was reduced in comparison to the Skua due to the turret replacing the fuselage fuel tanks of the Skua.

The Roc was issued to 800, 801 and 803 Naval Air Squadrons during 1939, supplementing the Skuas of all three units. In service, gunners and pilots found it difficult to co-ordinate their actions and on patrol Rocs had to return to their base or carrier over an hour earlier than the Skuas due to their reduced fuel capacity. 803 divested itself of Rocs (the Commanding Officer describing them as 'a constant hindrance') but both 800 and 801 squadrons took Rocs into action during the Norwegian campaign aboard HMS *Ark Royal,* but their inadequate performance rendered them unable to intercept any German aircraft.

Rocs were later used in concert with Skuas to cover the Dunkirk evacuation and it was during this operation that the Roc scored its sole confirmed 'kill', a Junkers Ju 88 on 28 May 1940. Rocs also strafed and bombed moored E-boats and attacked gun emplacements at Cap Gris-Nez.

The woeful performance and general clumsiness of the Roc saw its removal from operations by the mid-1940, but it soldiered on as an air-sea rescue aircraft, army co-operation aircraft and target-tug, serving into 1943 in the latter role.

Blackburn Roc

L3075 served with 806 squadron, one of relatively few units to use the Roc operationally. 806 Squadron flew fighter patrols and dive bombing attacks over the Dunkirk evacuation beaches with both Skuas and Rocs.

Blackburn Roc

Weight: (Maximum takeoff) 3606kg (7950lb)

Dimensions: Length: 10.85m (35ft 7in), Wingspan: 14.03m (46ft), Height: 3.68m (12ft 1in)

Powerplant: One 675kW (905hp) Bristol Perseus XII 9-cylinder air-cooled radial engine

Speed: 359km/h (223mph)

Range: 700km (435 miles)

Ceiling: 5486m (18000ft)

Crew: 2

Armament: Four 7.7mm (0.303in) Browning machine guns in Boulton Paul Type A power-operated dorsal turret; up to eight 14kg (30lb) bombs on underwing carriers

---

Fairey Fulmar

Despite the performance limitations imposed by its two-seat design, the Fulmar proved remarkably successful and shot down more enemy aircraft than any other Fleet Air Arm fighter.

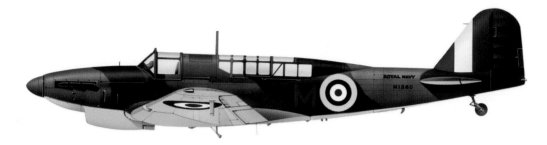

The Royal Navy entered World War II without a modern shipboard fighter. It was clear even before the conflict began that the Blackburn Skua lacked the necessary speed to intercept contemporary German bombers, let alone fighters, and the stop-gap biplane Gloster Sea Gladiator, although marginally faster, was conceptually obsolescent. The Admiralty was aware of the problem and had requested a modern monoplane fighter design in early 1938 although they were still wedded to the idea of the two-seater for carrier operations. The two-seat layout also allowed for the aircraft to readily take on reconnaissance and spotting duties and the Navy was always keen to utilize a multi-purpose aircraft given both the restricted space on carriers for different aircraft types and its limited budget.

Fighter adaption

Marcel Lobelle, chief designer at Fairey, proposed a fighter version of his pre-existing P.4/34 light bomber prototype that had demonstrated excellent performance and handling. The fact that the aircraft was stressed for dive bombing meant that it was already possessed of sufficient structural strength to withstand the

rigours of arrested carrier landings and catapult launches, and the bomber also boasted a great range capability, ideal for a naval fighter, and a stable, wide-track undercarriage that was well-suited for deck operations. The fact that the new fighter was a conversion of a pre-existing aircraft meant that valuable time and money could be saved in development. The proposal met with approval from the Admiralty and specification O.8/38 was written around Fairey's proposal. So great was the urgency attached to the project that 127 production aircraft were ordered at the same time as the specification was issued, there being no prototypes as such and the first and fifth aircraft off the production line were utilized for testing.

Clearance for service use was remarkably quick – the Fulmar first flew on 4 January 1940 and the first example was delivered to 778 squadron for deck landing trials on 10 May of the same year. Initially, production built up slowly and the first frontline unit received three Fulmars only by June, replacing three Blackburn Rocs of 886 squadron aboard HMS *Illustrious*. The Fulmar made its combat

Fairey Fulmar Mk.I

Fulmar N1860 is shown as it appeared when it was serving with 808 squadron at Dhekalia, Egypt in March or April 1941. Shore based Fulmar operations were relatively limited due to the aircraft's poor performance against German Messerschmitt Bf 109s and Vichy French Dewoitine D.520s.

Fairey Fulmar Mk.II

Weight: (Maximum takeoff) 4627kg (10,200lb)
Dimensions: Length: 12.24m (40ft 2in), Wingspan: 14.14m (46ft 4.5in), Height: 3.25m (10ft 8in)
Powerplant: One 970kW (1300hp) Rolls-Royce Merlin 30 V-12 liquid-cooled piston engine
Speed: 440km/h (272mph)
Range: 1255km (780 miles)
Ceiling: 8300m (27,200ft)
Crew: 2
Armament: Eight 7.7mm (0.303in) or four 12.7mm (0.5in) Browning machine guns fixed forward-firing in wings; up to 226kg (500lb) bombload

debut on 2 September 1940 when four Italian Savoia Marchetti SM.79 trimotor torpedo bombers and a Cant Z.501 flying boat were all shot down by Fulmars operating off *Illustrious* while on its way to join the Mediterranean Fleet. Production tempo increased in the autumn of 1940 and by the end of that year seven squadrons had converted or been formed on the type. From January 1941 production switched to the Mk.II variant that featured a more powerful Merlin 30 engine delivering an additional 198kW (265hp) that was sufficient to raise the maximum speed slightly and allow the carriage of extra equipment.

Many Mk.IIs featured the heavier armament of four 12.7mm (0.50in) Browning machine guns replacing the eight 7.7mm (0.303in) guns originally fitted, though some airframes featured an asymmetric arrangement of four 7.7mm (0.303) in one wing and two 12.7mm (0.50in) weapons in the other.

Service debut

Fulmars were very heavily engaged over the three years or so following their service debut, providing top cover for the Swordfish and Albacore torpedo bombers during the Battle of Cape Matapan, performing air interception and escort duties from carriers involved in escorting convoys to the Soviet Union and Malta, including the relentless action surrounding the siege-breaking convoy of Operation Pedestal, and formed part of the fighter force covering the Allied invasion of North Africa, Operation Torch. The type also saw considerable service from shore bases, flying as fighter bombers from the UK during 1942 as well as serving in the Western Desert and fighting the Japanese in

Malaya. At the high point of its service, 20 squadrons were flying the Fulmar and ultimately it flew from five fleet carriers and eight escort carriers, as well as a few that served as 'disposable' aircraft from CAM ships. In accordance with the multi-purpose nature of the original proposal, much use was made of the Fulmar as both a convoy escort and (relatively) high speed reconnaissance machine, in the former role external fuel tanks conferred the excellent patrol endurance of five and a half hours (with reserves); likewise its excellent range made it well suited for the latter.

Fulmar Is of 809 squadron lined up for take off on HMS *Victorious* for a squadron exercise in December 1941.

Second-line role

After the first Grumman Martlets arrived during 1942, the Fulmar was gradually replaced and transferred into second-line roles, serving until the end of the war as an advanced training machine and many Fleet Air Arm pilots would make their first deck landings on a carrier in the Fairey fighter. The Fulmar's spacious rear cockpit also saw it utilized as a high-speed courier aircraft, and the only example of the Fulmar

A heavily stained and weathered Fairey Fulmar II N4062 displays its distinctive slender profile. The lack of a rear gun troubled some observers, several of whom made up for this deficiency by taking along a Thompson sub-machine gun as an extemporized defensive weapon.

known to exist today (N1854, the first Fulmar to be built) survived because it was utilized by Fairey as a civil aircraft with the rear cockpit configured to carry two passengers. The final Fulmars to see frontline service were the NF Mk.II night fighters, of which 100 were converted from Mk.II airframes by fitting AI Mk.IV radar.

The three radar aerials fitted to each wing reduced the maximum speed of the already ponderous Fulmar by a further 32km (20mph) and no night kills are known to have been achieved by the aircraft – the closest any came was the final operational flight of a Fulmar when, on 8 February 1945, an NF Mk.II attempted to intercept a Ju 88 that

was shadowing convoy JW64 on its voyage to Murmansk. After chasing the German bomber for 90 minutes and managing to close to a mile and a half distance the radar set broke down and the Fulmar was compelled to return to HMS Campania. On landing the arrestor hook failed and the Fulmar crashed into the barrier without injury to the crew. This represented a rather ignominious end to the career of this profoundly useful aircraft, and the Royal Navy's most successful fighter of the war that had scored 112 victories during its career.

Stanley Orr was both the top-scoring Fulmar ace and British Naval pilot of World War II, having scored 12 of his 17 kills with the Fulmar.

Vought F4U Corsair

The Corsair was very fast but highly demanding to land on a carrier. Teething problems were eventually ironed out and the Corsair enjoyed a highly successful frontline career long into the jet age.

When the prototype XF4U-1 Corsair was rolled out in May 1939, it possessed the largest and most powerful engine, largest propeller and largest wing of any Naval fighter yet built and was undeniably impressive; but it is unlikely that anyone present would have realized that this purposeful looking aircraft would boast the longest production run of any US piston-engine fighter and become one of the greatest combat aircraft in history. Designed by Rex Beisel, it first flew on 29 May 1939, although testing was held up when the aircraft overturned following an emergency landing on a golf course. Flying again by the late summer of 1940, the XF4U-1 gained early fame by becoming the first US fighter to exceed 650km/h (400mph) in level flight. It also demonstrated a spectacular rate of climb and a terrific ceiling of 10,736m (35,200ft). On the other hand, the aircraft exhibited some unfortunate handling traits, not least the tendency to drop a wing when it reached touchdown speed, which was a portent of things to come.

As the XF4U-1 was put through the standard Navy tests an initial production batch of 584 aircraft was ordered on 3 March 1941, an enormous order by the standards of the time and reflecting the increasing likelihood the US would be involved in imminent war. The size of the order saw Vought seek associate contractors for Corsair production and both Brewster Aeronautical Corporation and Goodyear Aircraft Corporation signed up during November 1941, both of which would mass produce Corsairs as the F3A-1 and FG-1 respectively.

Heavy hitter

The first production aircraft appeared from Vought's new Dallas factory in June 1942. These differed significantly from the prototype as several changes had been introduced based on combat reports coming out of Europe, the most serious of which derived from the need to fit a heavier armament. The wing was therefore redesigned to accept three 12.7mm (0.5in) machine guns each side, the nose guns and associated synchronizing gear being discarded. This used up space in the wing that was being used for fuel that had to be moved to the fuselage. For centre of gravity reasons, the fuel

tank had to be placed above the wing structure, which meant the cockpit had to be moved 92cm (3ft) rearwards. This, coupled with the nose-high attitude required during an approach to a carrier, made for an extremely poor forward view, a criticism that would dog the Corsair for its entire operational life.

The Royal Navy's 1835 squadron was formed as a Corsair unit and was based at Brunswick Naval Air station in Maine for working up and deck landing training. This Corsair I, JT172, displays the distinctive 'birdcage' canopy typical of early Corsairs.

Vought Corsair Mk.I

Weight: (Maximum takeoff) 6350kg (14,000lb)
Dimensions: Length: 10.16m (33ft 4in), Wingspan: 12.5m (41ft), Height: 5.13m (16ft 10in)
Powerplant: One kW (3000hp) Pratt & Whitney R-2800-8 Double Wasp 14-cylinder air-cooled radial piston engine
Speed: 671km/h (417mph)
Range: 1633km (1015 miles)
Ceiling: 11,247m (36,900ft)
Crew: 1
Armament: Five 12.7mm (0.50in) Browning M2 machine guns fixed forward firing in wings

Vought Corsair Mk.IV

Pictured as it appeared in August 1945, this Corsair IV of 1850 squadron aboard HMS *Victorious* wears the standard USN high gloss overall sea blue finish retained by late war US-built British naval aircraft and displays the distinctive roundels adopted by the British Pacific Fleet.

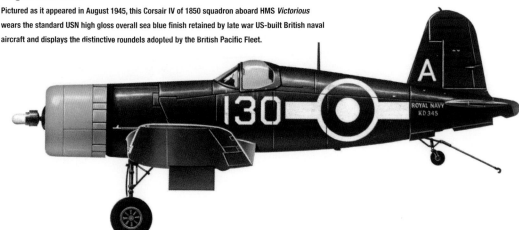

The aircraft had yet to undertake carrier trials when the first Corsair deliveries were received at the end of July 1942. Faced with an urgent need for a higher performance fighter than the F4F to combat Japanese forces in the Pacific, the decision was taken to give Marine Corps units priority for F4U-1 deliveries for land-based operations. Accordingly, the first unit to receive Corsairs was Marine Corps unit VMF-124 in September 1942 and they would be the first to take the F4U into combat when they were dispatched to support the beleaguered US forces on Guadalcanal in February 1943. Despite their inexperience (the pilots each had an average of 20 hours experience on the type), the Marine pilots rapidly established air superiority over the islands. The success of the Corsair was evident and within six months all South Pacific based Marine Corps fighter units would be equipped with the F4U.

Carrier trials

Meanwhile the Corsair was undergoing carrier trials aboard USS *Core* that confirmed the difficulties of deck landing the F4U. Both the poor visibility issue and the wing-drop tendency when near the stall were compounded by unfortunately stiff shock absorbers in the undercarriage that resulted in the aircraft bouncing back up after the wheels touched the carrier deck, leading potentially to the hook missing all the arrestor wires and an inevitable crash. Even if this were not to occur, the bouncing tendency combined with the low-profile canopy of early Corsairs often resulted in the pilot's head being violently battered against the inside of the canopy. It has often been stated that the Corsair failed its carrier qualification tests and that it took the British Fleet Air Arm to develop landing techniques for it but this is a myth. Three USN units had carrier-qualified before the Royal Navy even started to receive Corsairs. Nonetheless, the fact that the F4U was acknowledged to be a difficult aircraft for the average pilot to deck land, particularly when compared to the docile Hellcat, undoubtedly contributed to the decision, taken primarily to simplify logistics of spare parts supply, to equip land-based Marine-corps units with Corsairs and operate Hellcats from carriers.

Vought Corsair Mk.IV

Weight: (Maximum takeoff) 6350kg (14,000lb)
Dimensions: Length: 10.16m (33ft 4in), Wingspan: 12.5m (41ft), Height: 5.13m (16ft 10in)
Powerplant: One 1492kW (2000hp) Pratt & Whitney R-2800-8W Double Wasp 18-cylinder air cooled radial piston engine
Speed: 671km/h (417mph)
Range: 1633km (1015 miles)
Ceiling: 11,247m (36,900ft)
Crew: 1
Armament: Five 12.7mm (0.50in) Browning M2 machine guns fixed forward firing in wings: up to 907kg (2000lb) bombload or six 127mm (5in) rockets

With the US Navy threatening to drop the F4U from its carrier inventory in favour of the Hellcat, urgent measures were taken by Vought to improve the F4U's deck manners. From the 759th aircraft onwards a raised cockpit canopy was fitted improving pilot view, aircraft so equipped being retrospectively designated F4U-1A. A small spoiler was fitted to the starboard wing to prevent wing drop near the stall, the tail wheel leg was lengthened to lower the nose angle on the ground and the shock absorbers were altered to make

Vought F4U-2
'Shirley June' was an early example of the rare F4U-2 radar equipped night fighter variant. Based on Kawajalein Atoll in 1944, this aircraft served with VMF(N)-532, the second Marine Corps night fighter unit, and the first such unit to fly the Corsair.

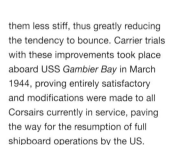

them less stiff, thus greatly reducing the tendency to bounce. Carrier trials with these improvements took place aboard USS *Gambier Bay* in March 1944, proving entirely satisfactory and modifications were made to all Corsairs currently in service, paving the way for the resumption of full shipboard operations by the US.

British usage

However, the British Royal Navy had already been regularly operating the Corsair from carriers since mid-1943. British Corsairs were easily distinguished as they had 22cm (8in) clipped from each wingtip to allow the aircraft to fit in the hangar decks of Royal Navy carriers, this modification also improving the stall characteristics of the fighter. The operational debut of the Corsair in British hands occurred during April 1944 in both Europe and

the Pacific, 1834 squadron forming part of the fighter cover for Barracudas attacking the *Tirpitz* while aircraft from HMS *Illustrious* escorted strike aircraft attacking the refineries on Sabang, Sumatra. Initial Corsairs were designated Corsair I with raised cockpit versions becoming the Corsair II. F3As from Brewster, of which the Royal Navy would receive over half produced, and Goodyear FG-1s were referred to as Corsair IIIs and IVs respectively.

Night fighter

Further development concentrated on improving the Corsair's versatility and performance, the F4U-2 was a night-fighter variant first that appeared during January 1943 and featured an AN/APS-6 radar in a pod on the starboard wingtip. The F4U-3 was a turbo-supercharged version that did not see production, but the F4U-4, featuring the R2800-18W

Vought F4U-2
Weight: (Maximum takeoff) 6350kg (14,000lb)
Dimensions: Length: 10.16m (33ft 4in), Wingspan: 12.5m (41ft), Height: 5.13m (16ft 10in)
Powerplant: One kW (3000hp) Pratt & Whitney R-2800-8 Double Wasp 14-cylinder air-cooled radial piston engine
Speed: 671km/h (417mph)
Range: 1633km (1015 miles)
Ceiling: 11,247m (36900ft)
Crew: 1
Armament: Five 12.7mm (0.50in) Browning M2 machine guns fixed forward firing in wings

water-boosted engine with a four-bladed propeller, began to enter service in early 1945, representing the most formidable wartime Corsair.

By this time, however, the Corsair was seeing more use as a ground attack asset than an air superiority fighter. Nonetheless, Goodyear

Vought F4U-1D

The distinctive tail marking of this F4U-1D of VBF-83 denotes that it was operating from USS *Essex*. VBF-83 would operate from *Essex* from March 1945 until the end of the conflict in September.

developed a variant, with a one 2237kW (3000hp) Pratt & Whitney R-4360 Wasp Major and a teardrop canopy specifically for combating low level kamikaze attackers as the F2G, demonstrating spectacular speed, but although production was ordered, the end of the war saw the project's cancellation.

Post-war developments were the F4U-5 with a more powerful engine, the F4U-7 developed for the French Navy that fought over Vietnam (French Indochina) and the AU-1, a dedicated attack variant for the Marine Corps. Corsairs were produced until 1952 and saw much service over Korea and subsequently with many other nations. A Honduran F4U-5 achieved the last confirmed 'kill' by a piston-engine fighter when it shot down an El Salvadorean F-51 Mustang and two FG-1s in July 1969. Honduras finally retired the last Corsairs in frontline service in 1981.

Vought F4U-1A Corsair

Weight: (Maximum takeoff) 6350kg (14,000lb)
Dimensions: Length: 10.16m (33ft 4in), Wingspan: 12.5m (41ft), Height: 5.13m (16ft 10in)
Powerplant: One 1492kW (2000hp) Pratt & Whitney R-2800-8 Double Wasp 14-cylinder air-cooled radial piston engine
Speed: 671km/h (417mph)
Range: 1633km (1015 miles)
Ceiling: 11,247m (36,900ft)
Crew: 1
Armament: Six 12.7mm (0.50in) M2 Browning machine guns fixed forward-firing in wings

Vought F4U-1A

This Corsair was operating over Bougainville in November 1943 with VF-17, the 'Jolly Rogers'. It was flown by Frederick 'Big Jim' Streig who was to shoot down six Japanese aircraft by the end of the conflict, all with the F4U.

Cutaway key

1 Spinner
2 Three-bladed Hamilton Standard constant-speed propeller
3 Reduction gear housing
4 Nose ring
5 Pratt & Whitney R-2800-8W Double Wasp 18-cylinder two-row engine
6 Exhaust pipes
7 Hydraulically operated cowling
8 Fixed cowling panels
9 Wing leading-edge unprotected integral fuel tank, capacity 62 US gal (235 litres)
10 Truss-type main spar
11 Leading-edge rib structure
12 Starboard navigation light
13 Wingtip
14 Wing structure
15 Wing ribs
16 Wing outer-section (fabric skinning aft of main spar)
17 Starboard aileron
18 Ammunition boxes (maximum total capacity 2,350 rounds)
19 Aileron trim tab
20 Aerial mast
21 Forward bulkhead
22 Oil tank, capacity 28 US gal (106 litres)
23 Oil tank forward armour plate
24 Fire suppressor cylinder
25 Supercharger housing
26 Exhaust trunking
27 Blower assembly
28 Engine support frame
29 Engine control runs
30 Wing main spar carry-through structure
31 Engine support attachment
32 Upper cowling deflection plate (0.1- in/ 0.25-cm aluminium)
33 Fuel filler cap
34 Fuselage main fuel tank, capacity 237 US gal (897 litres)
35 Upper longeron
36 Fuselage forward frames
37 Rudder pedals
38 Heelboards
39 Control column
40 Instrument panel
41 Reflector sight
42 Armoured-glass windshield
43 Rear-view mirror
44 Rearward-sliding cockpit canopy
45 Handgrip
46 Headrest
47 Pilot's head and back armour
48 Canopy frame
49 Pilot's seat
50 Engine control quadrant
51 Trim tab control wheels
52 Wing folding lever
53 Centre/aft fuselage bulkhead
54 Radio shelf
55 Radio installation
56 Canopy track
57 Bulkhead
58 Aerial lead-in
59 Aerial mast

60 Aerials
61 Heavy sheet skin plating
62 Dorsal identification light
63 Longeron
64 Control runs
65 Aft fuselage structure
66 Compass installation
67 Lifting tube
68 Access/inspection panels
69 Fin/fuselage forward attachment
70 Starboard tailplane
71 Elevator balance
72 Fin structure
73 Inspection panels
74 Rudder balance
75 Aerial stub
76 Rudder upper hinge
77 Rudder structure
78 Diagonal bracing

79 Rudder trim tab
80 Trim tab actuating rod
81 Access panel
82 Rudder post
83 Tailplane end rib
84 Elevator control runs
85 Fixed fairing root
86 Elevator trim tabs (port and starboard)
87 Tail cone
88 Rear navigation light
89 Port elevator
90 Elevator balance
91 Port tailplane structure
92 Arrestor hook (stowed)
93 Tail section frames
94 Fairing
95 Tailwheel (retracted)
96 Arrestor hook (lowered)
97 Tailwheel/hook doors

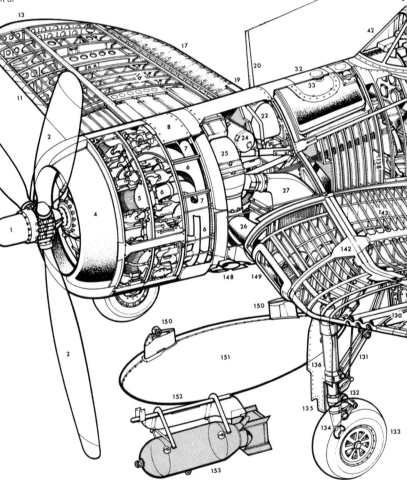

F4U-1A Corsair

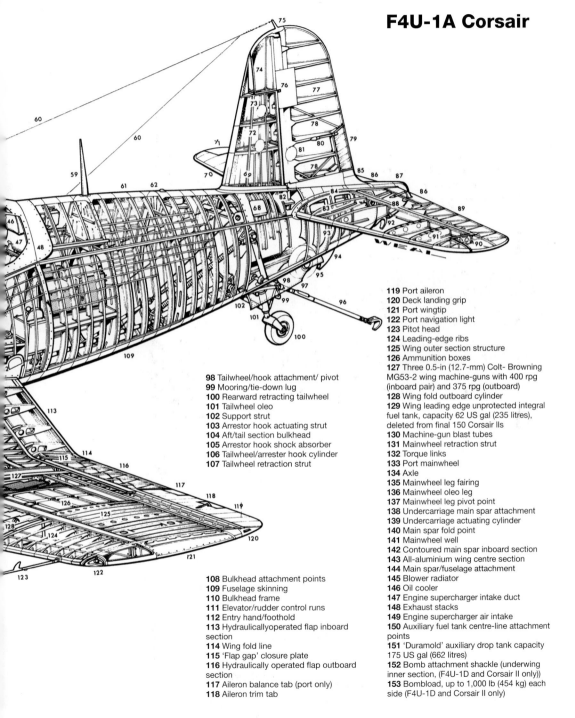

98 Tailwheel/hook attachment/ pivot
99 Mooring/tie-down lug
100 Rearward retracting tailwheel
101 Tailwheel oleo
102 Support strut
103 Arrestor hook actuating strut
104 Aft/tail section bulkhead
105 Arrestor hook shock absorber
106 Tailwheel/arrester hook cylinder
107 Tailwheel retraction strut

108 Bulkhead attachment points
109 Fuselage skinning
110 Bulkhead frame
111 Elevator/rudder control runs
112 Entry hand/foothold
113 Hydraulicallyoperated flap inboard section
114 Wing fold line
115 'Flap gap' closure plate
116 Hydraulically operated flap outboard section
117 Aileron balance tab (port only)
118 Aileron trim tab

119 Port aileron
120 Deck landing grip
121 Port wingtip
122 Port navigation light
123 Pitot head
124 Leading-edge ribs
125 Wing outer section structure
126 Ammunition boxes
127 Three 0.5-in (12.7-mm) Colt- Browning MG53-2 wing machine-guns with 400 rpg (inboard pair) and 375 rpg (outboard)
128 Wing fold outboard cylinder
129 Wing leading edge unprotected integral fuel tank, capacity 62 US gal (235 litres), deleted from final 150 Corsair IIs
130 Machine-gun blast tubes
131 Mainwheel retraction strut
132 Torque links
133 Port mainwheel
134 Axle
135 Mainwheel leg fairing
136 Mainwheel oleo leg
137 Mainwheel leg pivot point
138 Undercarriage main spar attachment
139 Undercarriage actuating cylinder
140 Main spar fold point
141 Mainwheel well
142 Contoured main spar inboard section
143 All-aluminium wing centre section
144 Main spar/fuselage attachment
145 Blower radiator
146 Oil cooler
147 Engine supercharger intake duct
148 Exhaust stacks
149 Engine supercharger air intake
150 Auxiliary fuel tank centre-line attachment points
151 'Duramold' auxiliary drop tank capacity 175 US gal (662 litres)
152 Bomb attachment shackle (underwing inner section, (F4U-1D and Corsair II only))
153 Bombload, up to 1,000 lb (454 kg) each side (F4U-1D and Corsair II only)

33

Tail identification
The US Navy introduced letter codes
for its aircraft in July 1945, replacing
the geometrical symbols used since
January of the same year.

Vought F4U-5 Corsair fighters From USS *Tarawa* (CV-40) fly in formation over the
Mediterranean, 15 December 1952.

Vought F4U-5N

Weight: (Maximum takeoff) 6398kg (14,106lb)

Dimensions: 10.5m (34ft 7in), Wingspan: 12.49m
(41ft), Height: 4.49m (14ft 9in)

Powerplant: One 1790kW (2400hp) Pratt &
Whitney R-2800-32W Double Wasp 18-cylinder air
cooled radial piston engine

Speed: 756km/h (470mph)

Range: 1790km (1120 miles)

Ceiling: 11,247m (36,900ft)

Crew: 1

Armament: Four 20mm (0.79in) AN/M3 fixed
forward firing in wings; up to 1452kg (3200lb)
bombload or eight 127mm (5in) rockets

Vought F4U-5N Corsair, VMF(N)-513
One of the most significant combat aircraft
in history, the Corsair remained in production
from 1942 to 1953, the longest production run
of any piston-engine fighter. The F4U-5N was
one of the later versions and saw extensive
service over Korea.

Cockpit
Later Corsairs featured a raised seat and canopy to provide the pilot with a better view over the nose, the forward cowling was lowered by two degrees for the same reason. From the F4U-4 onwards, Corsairs featured a flat, bulletproof windscreen replacing the curved plexiglass of earlier models.

Armament
The Corsair had been fitted with four 20mm (0.8in) M-3 cannon starting with the F4U1C in mid 1943, but this armament was not initially popular and suffered from teething issues. The F4U-5N could also carry two 454kg (I,000lb) bombs or napalm tanks, eight 127mm (5in) HVAR rockets or eight 300mm (11.75in) Tiny Tim rockets.

Radar
The F4U-5N mounted the AN/APS-19 radar in a relatively large pod on the starboard wing. The AN/APS-19 was developed by Sperry towards the end of World War Two, entering service in 1946.

Hawker Sea Hurricane

A hurried conversion to answer a desperate need for a better fighter than the Fulmar, the Hawker Sea Hurricane enjoyed a surprisingly successful career, providing the Fleet Air Arm with a relatively modern fighter at its moment of greatest need.

During the 1940s, attacks on the vital Atlantic convoys by Focke Wulf Fw 200 Condors were beginning to become a serious threat, and even if the aircraft did not attack it could transmit details of a convoy's position to U-boats. The Fulmar that had entered service in the spring of 1940 possessed only a meagre performance advantage over the Condor, but to further exacerbate the problem by mid-1940 the Royal Navy had lost two of its seven carriers and was understandably reticent about committing any of the remaining vessels to convoy protection. Thus the stage was set for the Hurricane's debut at sea, which took place not from a carrier deck but from a crude catapult on a cargo ship. Standard RAF Hurricane Mk.Is that had recently been phased out of Fighter Command service, and were noticeably worn out, were overhauled, fitted with catapult spools and other comparatively minimal naval equipment by General Aircraft Ltd and called the Sea Hurricane Mk.Ia.

The Merchant Ship Fighter Unit, comprised of volunteer pilots from both the RAF and Navy, was hastily formed to fly these aircraft from Catapult Aircraft Merchant (CAM) ships. In the event of a German aircraft being sighted, the Sea Hurricane was fired off the catapult to either shoot down or drive off the intruder. The obvious downside to the scheme was that there was no means to recover the aircraft once it had completed its mission, the pilot could either bale out or ditch near the convoy and hope to be picked up.

Despite the inherent danger of this system, only one pilot was lost during CAM ship operations. Although only nine German aircraft are known to have been shot down by CAM ship Hurricanes, many more were driven off and the system effectively halted the use of Focke Wulf Fw 200 Condors over the North Sea.

Operation Pedestal

The Sea Hurricane was to appear in a more comprehensively navalized form as the Sea Hurricane Mk.Ib, of which 340 were converted, complete with arrestor hook and strengthened

Hawker Sea Hurricane Mk.Ib

Sea Hurricane Z7015 was originally built in Canada as a standard Hurricane. In the UK, the aircraft was modified into a Sea Hurricane and served with 880 Squadron. Today, Z7015 is part of the Shuttleworth Collection and is the world's only surviving airworthy Sea Hurricane.

structure to absorb the stresses of carrier landings. This was not the first Hurricane to operate from a carrier though. In the desperate evacuation from Norway during June 1940, the Hurricane Mk.Is of 46 Squadron RAF, with no arrestor hooks or any modification for carrier use save for slightly deflated tyres, were successfully landed on HMS *Glorious* by RAF pilots with no deck landing experience. This incident finally proved that there was no impediment to operating high performance single-seat fighters at sea.

The first examples of the truly carrier-capable Sea Hurricane Ib entered service in July 1941 and the first kill was scored on the last day of that month when a Dornier Do 18 was shot down by aircraft from HMS *Furious.* Subsequently seeing action from the Baltic, escorting convoys to Russia to the Indian Ocean and attacking Vichy forces in Madagascar, the Sea Hurricane was very active over the next two years.

The most notable action it engaged in was probably Operation Pedestal of August 1942, during which a very heavily escorted convoy of 14 fast merchant ships fought its way through to Malta with much needed supplies, not least a tanker full of aviation fuel.

Four fleet carriers were provided for the escort and most of the fighter force consisted of Sea Hurricanes. Attacked near constantly on its journey from Gibraltar the Sea Hurricanes saw much action and on 12 August Lieutenant Richard Cork became the only Royal Navy pilot to achieve 'ace in a day' status by shooting down five enemy aircraft.

The aircraft in which Cork achieved this feat is reputed to have been a Mk.Ib fitted with four 20mm (0.787in) cannon. That such a conversion existed is known but it is unclear if the aircraft was ever used for anything other than trials, the weight of the armament having a seriously deleterious effect on the Sea Hurricane's performance. However, the next Sea Hurricane variant was cannon-armed from the outset. The Sea Hurricane Mk.IIC was again a conversion from a standard RAF type, 81 airframes being diverted for naval use in May 1942. It featured both a quartet of 20mm (0.787in) Hispano cannon and a 1089kw (1460hp) Merlin XX engine, sufficient to propel it at the creditably high speed of 550 km/h (342mph). The Sea Hurricane IIC was available in time to see service during Operation Torch, the Allied invasion of North Africa, when around 40 operated

Hawker Sea Hurricane Mk.Ib
Weight: (Maximum takeoff) 3511kg (7740lb)
Dimensions: Length: 9.83m (32ft 4in), Wingspan: 12.2m (40ft), Height: 4m (13ft 1in)
Powerplant: One 954kW (1280hp) Rolls-Royce Merlin XX V-12 liquid-cooled piston engine
Speed: 505km/h (314mph)
Range: 1207km (750 miles)
Ceiling: 10,516m (34,500ft)
Crew: 1
Armament: Four 20mm (0.79in) Hispano cannon fixed forward-firing in wings

Hawker Sea Hurricane Mk.X
Another Canadian built aircraft, BW850 was built from scratch as a Sea Hurricane and intended to be supplied to the RN. This aircraft was, however, retained in Canada for service with 440 squadron RCAF.

off the escort carriers HMS *Biter*, *Avenger* and *Dasher*.

The final Sea Hurricane deliveries were made in August 1943, by which time the advent of the F6F Hellcat in US service suddenly made stocks of the F4F Wildcat/Martlet available for Royal Navy use as well as the potent but somewhat problematic Corsair. The last unit to fly the Sea Hurricane, 835 squadron aboard the escort carrier *Nairana*, converted to the Wildcat VI in September 1944.

Folding wings
During its career the Sea Hurricane never received folding wings. The possibility of designing a folding wing was studied during 1940 but the desperate need to get Hurricanes onto carriers as quickly as possible and concerns over the weight of such a system meant that it was abandoned. This would prove to be arguably the

greatest single problem with the Sea Hurricane, as only two carriers – HMS *Eagle* and *Ark Royal* – had deck lifts of sufficient size to stow the Hurricanes' hangar below deck and they had both been lost by August 1942. The newer *Illustrious* class fleet carriers had to store Sea Hurricanes on deck, in all weathers, and limited the amount that could be carried to only six or so aircraft. Serviceability rates were surprisingly good under the circumstances and attested to the durable nature of the Hurricane. In the words of pilot Eric Brown, "less likely a candidate for deployment aboard aircraft carriers as a naval single-seat fighter than the Hurricane could have been imagined... yet, legacy of parsimony, expediency and shortsightedness inflicted on British naval aviation (it) undoubtedly was, the Hurricane was to take to the nautical environment extraordinarily well."

Photographed in August 1942, Sea Hurricane Mk.Ib Z4039 was on the strength of 760 Squadron, No.1 Fleet Fighter Pool. This unit later became a training and conversion squadron for one of the Sea Hurricane's main replacements: the Vought Corsair.

Fairey Firefly

Superficially resembling the Fulmar, the Fairey Firefly was a considerably more powerful and formidable aircraft that saw much action during the last two years of war before enjoying a long post-war career.

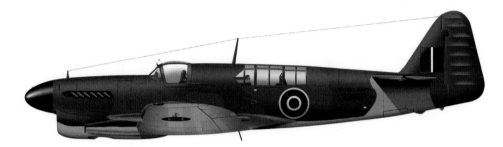

The specification that led to the Firefly was issued shortly before the war when the Royal Navy identified a need for both a single- and two-seat fighter. The single-seat requirement led to the Blackburn Firebrand, which was hugely delayed and ultimately saw only limited post-war service in a completely different role to that originally envisaged, but the Firefly, built to a seemingly outmoded two-seat concept, was to prove highly successful.

Using the Fulmar as a basis, Fairey's chief designer H.E. 'Charlie' Chaplin (who had succeeded Marcel Lobelle after he had left to set-up his own company) drew up a design based around the new Rolls-Royce Griffon engine, which had itself been designed at the behest of the Fleet Air Arm.

Maiden flight

The original specification for what became the Firefly featured a power-operated gun turret, but after the underwhelming combat performance of both the RAF's Boulton Paul Defiant and the Navy's own Blackburn Roc

this requirement was dropped and a new specification, N5.40, was written around Fairey's proposed design. Confident in the potential of the design and cognisant of the urgent need to replace the Fulmar (which had entered service the previous month), the Ministry of Aircraft Production ordered 200 'off the drawing board' after Fairey had presented a mock-up of the aircraft during June 1940 with the first three production machines intended for use as prototypes. Accordingly, the first Firefly took to the air on 22 December 1941.

Testing proved remarkably trouble-free, the most significant change made to the airframe before it was cleared for service being a switch from fabric to metal skinning on the ailerons and elevators to alleviate control heaviness and some handling issues. The change was successful but the Firefly would always require a significant physical effort to perform aerobatics, especially to a pilot used to the beautifully light controls of the Seafire. Nevertheless, the aircraft was considered agile, the patented Fairey-Youngman flaps

Fairey Firefly Mk I

The first production Fireflies such as Z2035 featured a low profile canopy but the restricted headroom this provided led to the introduction of a taller canopy that was fitted to the majority of Fireflies. The Firefly was a large and undeniably impressive aircraft.

Fairey Firefly Mk.I

Weight: (Maximum takeoff) 6375kg (14,054lb)
Dimensions: Length: 11.45m (37ft 7in), Wingspan: 13.55m (44ft 6in), Height: 4.15m (13ft 7in)
Powerplant: One 970kW (1735hp) Rolls-Royce Griffon IIB V-12 liquid-cooled piston engine
Speed: 509km/h (316mph)
Range: 2100km (1,305 miles)
Ceiling: 8535m (28,000ft)
Crew: 2
Armament: Four 20mm (0.79in) Hispano cannon fixed forward-firing in wings; up to 908kg (2000lb) bombload or eight 27kg (60lb) rockets

allowed for excellent low speed handling and during tests with the US Navy during 1944 the Firefly I was demonstrated to be able to out-turn the F6F Hellcat. However, with a top speed of 509km/h (316mph), the Firefly was undeniably slow. This was mainly as a result of the considerable size and weight imposed by the requirement to carry a second crew member and associated equipment, although the chin-mounted radiator also imposed a considerable drag penalty and the radiators were moved to a more aerodynamic position on the wing leading edge in the next major

production version, the F Mk.4.

Deck landing trials took place during the summer of 1943 on the fleet carrier HMS *Illustrious* before moving on to the smaller escort carrier *Pretoria Castle*. In October 1943 the first frontline Navy unit, 1770 squadron, after a working-up period flew the Firefly's first major combat mission on 17 July when the squadron took part in an attack on the German battleship *Tirpitz* anchored at Kåfjord in Norway. Further escort and strike missions along the Norwegian coastline kept European-based Fireflies busy for the remainder of the conflict.

This view of a post-war Firefly landing shows well the cleaned up nose sported by the Mk 4, 5 and 6 Fireflies. Twin radiators in the leading edge of the inner wings replaced the beard radiator sported by earlier variants.

Operation Meridian

The bulk of the Firefly's wartime career would take place in the Pacific, with 1770 squadron joining HMS *Indefatigable* in December 1944. Less than a month later the Fireflies would lead Operation Meridian, a successful series of strikes on Japanese-held oil refineries on Sumatra. This operation would also result in the Firefly's first air-to-air victories when two Nakajima Ki 43s were destroyed by Firefly pilots. The Firefly subsequently enjoyed a busy period of operations with the British Pacific Fleet, culminating in strikes on the Japanese mainland during the course of which the Firefly garnered a certain amount of fame by becoming the first British aircraft to fly over Tokyo. Encounters with Japanese aircraft would be relatively rare during the late war period but one pilot, Sub Lt Phil Stott, nonetheless managed to become an 'ace' on the type by scoring five victories.

Limited service

Development of a night fighter variant of the Firefly proved problematic. The purpose-built NF.II fitted British AI Mk.X radar that required a radome on each wing and a heavy generator, requiring the fuselage to be extended, which resulted in visibility and stability issues that saw production halted

after only 37 had been built. None saw service and nearly all were converted to standard Mk.Is. A simpler solution was utilized in the NF Mk.I, a conversion of the standard fighter with an American AN/APS-4 radar mounted in a fibreglass pod on a ventral rack. This saw some service over Europe before the end of the war but no successful interceptions were made. The type was sent to the Pacific but the war ended before it saw service. Eventually enough AN/APS-4 units became available for them to be fitted to day fighters as well, being designated FR.I (FR standing for Fighter-Reconnaissance). The first unit, 816 squadron, received FR.Is as a replacement for the Barracuda in July 1945 but saw no action before VJ Day.

Improved performance

Post-war, the aircraft saw much development and widespread service in its original role as well as a trainer, anti-submarine aircraft, target tug and drone controller. Post-war marks featured a more aerodynamic nose and clipped wings resulting in improved performance. Fireflies operated for the duration of the Korean war and were flying attack operations as late as 1962 in Royal Netherlands Navy service against Indonesian forces in Dutch New Guinea.

Fairey Firefly AS.5

Post-war, the Firefly's two seat configuration and relatively large size allowed it to be adapted for a swathe of new tasks. The AS.5 was optimized for the Anti-Submarine Warfare role.

Fairey Firefly AS.5

Weight: (Maximum takeoff) 7301kg (16,096lb)

Dimensions: Length: 11.56m (37ft 11in), Wingspan: 12.67m (41ft 7in), Height: 4.24m (13ft 11in)

Powerplant: One 1494kW (2004hp) Rolls-Royce Griffon 74 V-12 liquid-cooled piston engine

Speed: 621km/h (386mph)

Range: 1223km (760 miles)

Ceiling: 9723m (31,900ft)

Crew: 2

Armament: Four 20mm (0.79in) Hispano cannon fixed forward-firing in wings; up to 908kg (2000lb) bombload or 16 27kg (60lb) rockets

Supermarine Seafire

The most-produced British carrier fighter of World War II, the Seafire was a superlative aircraft in the air but ill-suited to deck landing. Despite this impediment it enjoyed widespread use and a long career.

The Supermarine Spitfire is the most famous British aircraft of World War II and probably of all time. For much of its career it was arguably the finest fighter aircraft in the world and as a result it is unsurprising that the Royal Navy should seek to take the aircraft to sea. As early as 1938 the Admiralty approached Fairey about the possibility of producing licence-built naval Spitfires, but the first definitive steps towards the production of a naval version of the aircraft took place the following year when Vickers-Supermarine began working with the Admiralty on designing an arrestor hook and folding wing system for the Spitfire. A fully navalized Spitfire-based design featuring Corsair-style inverted gull wings and powered by either the Rolls-Royce Griffon or Napier Sabre was proposed by Supermarine in 1939 to specification N.8/39, but was rejected.

After the war had begun, the campaign in Norway starkly demonstrated the limitations of the Royal Navy's then current fighters and led to the adoption of the Sea Hurricane, but the Air Ministry resisted calls to navalize the Spitfire, mainly due

to cost. By mid-1941 the Hurricane was considered obsolescent and sufficient quantities of Grumman Martlets could not be obtained from the US. A visit by Prime Minister Winston Churchill to HMS *Indomitable* in September revealed the sorry state of their fighter component and the following month he lent his personal support to Admiralty requests for Spitfires, and as a direct result work began apace.

Cannon armament

The first Seafire Ibs were minimal conversions of Mk.Vb Spitfires, the most obvious external change being the fitting of an a-frame arrestor hook under the rear fuselage, the extra weight of this item being balanced by two 12kg (26lb) lead weights either side of the engine. Internal changes included fitting a naval radio and an airspeed indicator calibrated in knots. Carrier trials aboard HMS *Illustrious* began in January 1942, leading to an initial assessment of the Seafire's deck landing characteristics as satisfactory, although concern was raised about

Supermarine Seafire LF Mk.III

Seen here with its under-fuselage arrestor hook deployed, PP979 was serving with 807 Squadron aboard HMS *Hunter* in the Indian Ocean. This aircraft was written off when it missed all the arrestor wires and hit the barrier on 26 June 1945; the pilot, Sub Lt Logie was uninjured.

Supermarine Seafire F Mk III
Weight: (Maximum takeoff) 3280kg (7232lb)
Dimensions: Length: 9.2m (30ft 3in), Wingspan: 11.23m (36ft 10in), Height: 3.49m (11ft 6in)
Powerplant: One 1182kW (1585hp) Rolls-Royce Merlin 55 V-12 liquid-cooled piston engine
Speed: 578km/h (359mph)
Range: 748km (465 miles)
Ceiling: 11,000m (36,000ft)
Crew: 1
Armament: Two 20mm (0.79in) Hispano cannons and four 12.7mm (0.5in) Browning machine guns fixed forward-firing in wings; up to 226kg (500lb) bombload or eight 27kg (60lb) rockets under wing

---

the long nose adversely affecting visibility on approach. Such was the rush to get the Seafire into service that by the time the formal specification and contract for production of the aircraft had been issued in August 1942, most of the initial 48 Seafires had already been delivered.

At the same time, work had been progressing on the development of the Seafire II, a slightly more thoroughly navalized aircraft featuring catapult spools to allow the aircraft to be catapult launched if necessary. These aircraft were built from scratch rather than converted from existing airframes, although it was still very much an adaptation of the Spitfire V. The aircraft was known as the Seafire Mk.IIc, the 'c' denoting cannon armament fitted in the Supermarine 'universal' wing. It is worth noting that the Fleet Air Arm also made use of many 'hooked Spitfires' that were standard ex-RAF Spitfires fitted with an arrestor hook but lacking any other naval equipment. These were used solely for training and were never referred to as Seafires.

First action

The first unit to convert to Seafires, 807 squadron, embarked with their aircraft on HMS *Furious* in August. A measure of the urgency with which the Seafire was required can be gauged by the fact that by the end of September a further four units had re-equipped with the aircraft with more to follow. The Seafire's combat debut would have to wait until the Operation Torch landings, during which it provided air cover and scored its initial aerial victories, the first on 8 November 1942 when a Vichy French Martin 167 was shot down.

On operations the Seafire had inherited the Spitfire's outstanding handling in the air, but was gaining a reputation for fragility on deck. The aircraft possessed a gentle stall, an unfortunate trait in a carrier aircraft that function best when they can be firmly stalled onto the carrier deck, and often tended to float over the arrestor wires

to crash into the barrier. Should all go well and an arrestor wire be caught, the position of the hook under the fuselage resulted in a sharp nose-down pitch as the aircraft decelerated. This, combined with the Spitfire's minimal airscrew clearance, caused the propeller blades to 'peck' the deck and render the aircraft unserviceable. Even if a pilot managed to avoid those two pitfalls, the undercarriage was relatively weak and prone to collapse. These issues came to a head during the Salerno landings when low windspeed over the deck, poor visibility and inexperience exacerbated the Seafire's deck landing issues to result in 73 aircraft from the

The Rolls-Royce Griffon engine gave the Seafire a useful increase in power over the Merlin originally fitted, though at the cost of further degradation of the Seafire's already problematic carrier landing characteristics. The pilot can be seen making a hurried exit from this stricken Seafire XVII.

original force of 105 lost or seriously damaged to non-combat causes over the course of three days. Nonetheless, the Seafire's airborne performance was sufficiently good enough to persist in its use and attempt to mitigate the worst of its deck landing issues.

Folding wings

Meanwhile, work to provide the Seafire with a folding wing had been carried out, Supermarine and the Ministry of Aircraft Production collaborating on the design. The system adopted was unusual among British fighters in that the wings folded vertically upward to allow clearance within the limited height of the standard British carrier hangar, the wingtips folded separately, resulting in a 'Z' form when folded. The first production Mk.IIc was rebuilt with folding wings in December 1942 and, remarkably, the new design was only 8.6kg (19lb) heavier than the standard wing it replaced.

Flight trials were undertaken in January 1943 and the aircraft ordered into production as the Seafire Mk.III

Supermarine Seafire Mk.III (Hybrid)

About 30 or so 'hybrid' aircraft were built by Westland that featured the Merlin 55 and four blade propeller of the Seafire III but the non-folding wings and three-pipe exhaust of the IIc. Seafire III (Hybrid) LR792 was serving on the escort carrier HMS *Battler* in the Indian Ocean in June 1944.

with deliveries beginning in April. Three subtypes were produced, the standard F Mk.III and fighter-reconnaissance FR Mk.III that featured provision for cameras in the rear fuselage were both powered by the Rolls-Royce Merlin 55, but the L Mk.III utilized the Merlin 55M driving a four-blade propeller and was intended for low-altitude operations. By now deck landing issues had been improved, although the Seafire was still more accident prone than the US-built fighters. Most of the Mk III's service took place with the British Pacific Fleet where the combat effectiveness of the Seafire III was improved by the adaptation at unit level of 90-gallon Kittyhawk drop tanks to extend the aircraft's somewhat minimal range. The Seafire was increasingly used for ground attack of shore targets but it proved effective against the dwindling numbers of Japanese aircraft, indeed the last confirmed air-to air-victory of the war fell to the guns of Sub Lieutenant J.G. Murphy's Seafire L Mk.III operating from HMS *Indefatigable* on the morning of 15 August 1945.

Towards the end of the war development had concentrated on getting a Rolls-Royce Griffon-powered Seafire onto the Royal Navy's carriers, but the Seafire Mk.XV just failed to enter service before VJ Day. This may have been something of a blessing, as the Seafire XV developed an appalling

reputation due to its potentially uncontrollable swing on takeoff and inadequate undercarriage that was prone to collapse (it utilized the same landing gear as the Seafire III but weighed considerably more). Handling problems were experienced not just when deck landing but, for the first time, during normal flight, resulting in numerous accidents and groundings.

Despite this it served with both the Royal Navy and Royal Canadian Navy. The problems led to the rapid development of the much improved Mk.XVII (later F 17), which featured a bubble canopy for the first time before the definitive FR Mk.47 entered service in 1948. This variant would see combat over Malaya and Korea before being phased out in the mid-1950s.

Supermarine Seafire F Mk III

Weight: (Maximum takeoff) 3280kg (7232lb)
Dimensions: Length: 9.2m (30ft 3in), Wingspan: 11.23m (36ft 10in), Height: 3.49m (11ft 6in)
Powerplant: One 1182kW (1585hp) Rolls-Royce Merlin 55 V-12 liquid-cooled piston engine
Speed: 578km/h (359mph)
Range: 748km (465 miles)
Ceiling: 11000m (36,000ft)
Crew: 1
Armament: Two 20mm (0.79in) Hispano cannons and four 12.7mm (0.5in) Browning machine guns fixed forward-firing in wings; up to 226kg (500lb) bombload or eight 27kg (60lb) rockets under wing

Blackburn Firebrand

Despite flying for the first time in February 1942, the unavailability of the Napier Sabre engine, a change in its intended role and slow development saw the Firebrand's service entry delayed until September 1945.

Blackburn Firebrand TF Mk.IV

One of the first Firebrands to see squadron service, EK613 was on the strength of 813 Squadron, the only unit ever to operate the Mk.IV, in mid-1946. These aircraft were replaced by the TF Mk.V in 1948 which 813 would operate until the Firebrand's replacement by the Westland Wyvern in 1953.

The Firebrand was originally designed to Specification N.8/39 that called for a two-seat fighter to replace the Skua, Roc and Fulmar but the two-seat requirement was dropped as a result of operational experience in the Norwegian campaign.

The design was modified into a large, high-performance, single-seat carrier interceptor powered by the new Napier Sabre 24-cylinder engine and armed with four 20mm (0.79in) cannon, and the prototype flew for the first time on 27 February 1942. Carrier trials were undertaken during February 1943 aboard HMS *Illustrious* but later that year the Ministry of Aircraft Production (MAP) decreed that all Sabre production was reserved for the Hawker Typhoon. This and the entry into FAA service of new American fighters and the Supermarine Seafire effectively ended the Firebrand's career as a carrier interceptor before it had even begun.

Keen to avoid wasting the work that had been expended to bring the Firebrand to this stage, the MAP suggested converting it into a strike aircraft able to carry either a torpedo or bombs. Blackburn widened the centre section of the wing by 39cm (15in) to allow clearance for a torpedo between the undercarriage legs, and in this form the aircraft was redesignated the TF.II (for Torpedo Fighter). Only 12 TF.IIs were built due to the ongoing unavailability of the Sabre, so Blackburn redesigned the aircraft to accept the Bristol Centaurus radial engine as the TF.III, 27 examples of which were produced before the improved TF.IV flew in May 1945. This would form the equipment of the first operational Firebrand squadron on 1 September 1945. Despite being a difficult aircraft to deck land due to the poor view over the nose, the unpopular Firebrand would remain in frontline service until 1953.

Blackburn Firebrand TF.IV

Weight: (Maximum takeoff) 7360kg (16,227lb)
Dimensions: Length: 12m (39ft 1in), Wingspan: 15.62m (51ft 4in), Height: 4.05m (13ft 3in)
Powerplant: One 1,865kW (2,500hp) Bristol Centaurus IX 18-cylinder air-cooled radial engine
Speed: 560km/h (350mph)
Range: 2000km (1,250 miles) with external tanks
Ceiling: 11,804m (38,700ft)
Crew: 1
Armament: Four 20mm (0.79in) Hispano Mk.II cannon in wings; up to two 454kg (1000lb) bombs under wings or one 840kg (1,850lb) 457mm (18in) Mk XVII torpedo under fuselage

Grumman F6F Hellcat

Credited with more combat victories than any other carrier fighter in history, the large and rugged F6F Hellcat effectively established the US Navy's aerial ascendency over their Japanese foes.

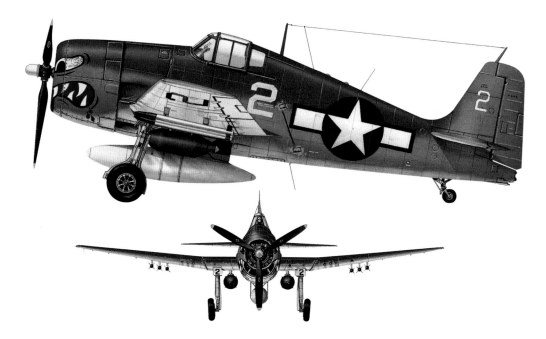

During 1939 and 40, aware of the threat posed by modern high-performance aircraft being developed in Japan, the US Navy sought to procure a fighter with still better characteristics than the F4F Wildcat then under development. The Vought F4U Corsair appeared to offer excellent performance but early testing was not progressing as well as the Navy would have liked, and it was considered prudent to develop an alternative fighter as a back-up to the Corsair. As a result, in June 1941 the Navy ordered two prototypes of an 'improved F4F'. The original plan was to fit the Wright R-2600 Cyclone in the F4F airframe but the Grumman design team, led by Leroy Grumman himself, felt that the requirement would be much better

answered by an entirely new design. This approach carried the risk of delay, but in the event herculean efforts by Grumman saw the new aircraft in combat a mere 14 months after the prototype's first flight.

Heavy fighter

The F6F as it emerged was considerably larger than the Wildcat it was intended to replace, possessing a loaded weight some 60 per cent greater than the earlier aircraft. The weight increase necessitated the use of a larger wing – indeed, the wing area of the F6F was the largest of any World War II single engine US fighter. In typical Grumman fashion the aircraft boasted immense structural strength

Grumman F6F-3 Hellcat

Large examples of 'nose art' remained relatively rare on naval aircraft throughout the war, the F6Fs of VF-27 were a notable exception, utilizing the distinctive 'Hellcat grin' formed by the inlets below the engine to great effect. This F6F-3 was serving aboard USS *Princeton* in 1944.

and in service would garner an enviable reputation for its ability to absorb punishment and remain airborne. Considerable attention was paid to pilot protection and 96kg (212lb) of the F6F's empty weight consisted of armour. This was in marked contrast to the design philosophy of the F6F's principal foe, the Mitsubishi A6M 'Zero', which sacrificed protection to achieve the best possible performance. Some consideration was given at Grumman to pursuing a similar approach but ultimately it was felt the loss of versatility and increased vulnerability that would result from this design was unacceptable.

Nonetheless, initial combat reports from Naval aviators who had clashed with Zeros revealed that the F6F would require the best speed and climb rate possible. At Grumman doubts were raised as to the wisdom of relying solely on the R-2600 Cyclone intended for the

Grumman F6F-3 Hellcat
Alexander Vraciu was a notable pilot with VF-16, the fourth most successful USN pilot of the war with 19 victories, all claimed whilst flying Hellcats, including this F6F-3 during the spring of 1944. On 19 June 1944, Vraciu shot down six Yokosuka D4Y dive bombers within the space of eight minutes.

XF6F-1 as development of the engine was beginning to lag behind that of Pratt & Whitney's R-2800 Double Wasp, which was offering a 1491kw (2000hp) potential against the Cyclone's 1268kw (1700hp). Grumman therefore obtained Navy approval to fit the R-2800 to the second prototype, designated XF6F-3, the designation XF6F-2 being reserved for a variant powered by a turbo-supercharged R-2800 that was briefly tested in January 1944 but progressed no further.

Flight trials
The Cyclone-powered prototype XF6F-1 flew for the first time on 26 June 1942 with the XF6F-3 following it into the air on 30 July. By the time of the first flight the R-2800 had been confirmed as the powerplant of choice and large-scale production had been ordered as the F6F-3 Hellcat on 23 May 1942 before the prototype had even flown. Flight trials were highly satisfactory, what few shortcomings there were being eradicated in the production standard machines that differed from the prototype externally only in the elimination of the propeller spinner and a change in the design of the undercarriage wheel fairings. Carrier acceptance trials were a little

more problematic as the arrestor hook was torn out of an early production F6F before a second landing incident resulted in the failure of the entire rear fuselage. Structural strengthening was rapidly undertaken and no further trouble was encountered. The first squadron to fly the F6F-3 was VF-9, with initial deliveries beginning in January 1943, the unit embarking on USS *Essex* during the spring of that year. On 31 August VF-5 aboard USS *Yorktown* took the F6F-3 into combat for the first time as part of the strike force attacking Japanese positions on Marcus Island. At roughly the same

Grumman F6F-3 Hellcat
Weight: (Maximum takeoff) 6000kg (13,217lbs)
Dimensions: Length: 10.17m (33ft 4in), Wingspan: 13.08m (42ft 10in), Height: 4.4m (14ft 5in)
Powerplant: One 149kW (2000hp) Pratt & Whitney R-2800-10 Double Wasp two row 18-cylinder air-cooled radial piston engine
Speed: 600km/h (373mph)
Range: 1755km (1090 miles)
Ceiling: 11,438m (37,500ft)
Crew: 1
Armament: Six 12.7mm (0.5in) Browning AN/M2 machine guns fixed forward-firing in wings; up to 907kg (2000lb) bombload or six 127mm (5in) rockets

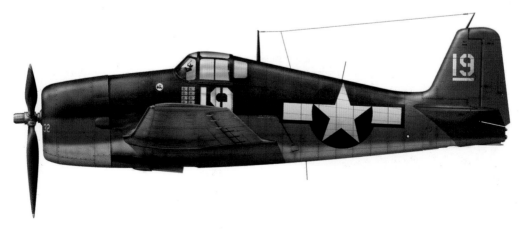

time the Royal Navy began to receive F6F-3s, designated Hellcat I, as part of lend-lease arrangements, the name 'Tarpon' having been initially allocated but dropped in favour of the American name before the aircraft entered service. The first Hellcats were supplied to 800 squadron on 1 July 1943, replacing the Sea Hurricane, and began their career in British hands with anti-shipping missions along the Norwegian coast before serving as escort for Barracudas attacking the battleship *Tirpitz,* an action that saw three Hellcats shooting down a German fighter apiece. However, most British Hellcat operations would take place in the Pacific.

Grumman F6F-5 Hellcat

Weight: (Maximum takeoff) 6002kg (13,221lb)
Dimensions: Length: 10.17m (33ft 4in), Wingspan: 13.08m (42ft 10in), Height: 4.4m (14ft 5in)
Powerplant: One 149kW (2000hp) Pratt & Whitney R-2800-10 Double Wasp two row 18-cylinder air-cooled radial piston engine
Speed: 600km/h (373mph)
Range: 2606km (1620 miles) with external fuel tank
Ceiling: 11,438m (37,500ft)
Crew: 1
Armament: Six 12.7mm (0.5in) Browning AN/M2 machine guns fixed forward-firing in wings; up to 1814kg (4000lb) bombload or six 127mm (5in) rockets or two 298mm (11.75in) Tiny Tim rockets

Night-fighter variant

Production built up rapidly at Grumman, with 2555 F6Fs constructed by the end of 1943 and conversion of F4F units to the new fighter proceeded quickly. In combat against the Japanese, the F6F proved even more formidable than its forebear and its excellent deck landing qualities and huge strength endeared it to pilots. During 1943, work was undertaken to adapt the Hellcat to both the reconnaissance and night-fighting roles. The former resulted in the F6F-3P high-altitude photo-reconnaissance version with cameras fitted in the fuselage directly behind the pilot. The night fighter required a rather more extensive modification, mounting a fairly large pod on the starboard wing containing the AN/APS-6 radar unit. The cockpit featured red lighting to reduce glare and a radar altimeter was fitted. The outer plexiglass windscreen was removed to cut down on reflections and landing lights were installed. Designated F6F-3N, 149 of the night-fighter variant were produced, entering service during February 1944 with VF(N)-76 aboard USS *Yorktown* and achieving their first victory during the same month.

Few changes were made to the basic Hellcat over its production life but the desire to maximize the speed performance of the aircraft saw the appearance of an aerodynamically cleaned-up version of the F6F-3 during January 1944, which achieved a speed of 660km/h (410mph) at 6405m (21,000ft). A new production standard incorporating some of the improvements of this aircraft went into production during April 1944 as the F6F-5 and was in widespread service by the late summer.

The principal differences were a new closer-fitting engine cowling, the deletion of the windows aft of the cockpit canopy and the removal of the curved front windscreen. Provision was made for the first time for the aircraft to carry underwing stores and in some later production F6F-5s two 20mm (0.79in) cannon replaced two of the standard 12.7mm (0.5in) machine guns.

In total, 7870 F6F-5s were built, including a few F6F-5P reconnaissance versions and 1434

Grumman F6F-5 Hellcat

VF-20 were deployed aboard USS *Enterprise* from August to November 1944. This Hellcat was flown by Leo Bob McUddin, who scored a total of five victories during the war, all achieved on this single combat tour.

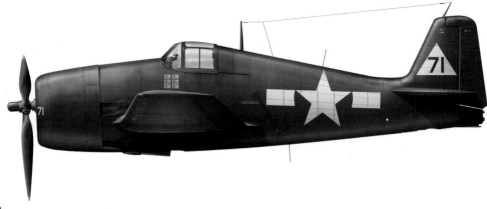

of the F6F-5N night-fighter version that featured the same wing mounted AN/APS-6 radar pod as the F6F-3N described above. An F6F-6 version, with a more powerful Double Wasp and the fastest of all the Hellcats, never entered production before all production was terminated on VJ Day.

After the war the Hellcat lingered in reserve squadrons for a few years, the last combat usage being as a guided missile. Explosive-laden F6F-5K remote-controlled flying bombs were used against targets in North Korea during the summer of 1952.

The Royal Navy acquired 935 F6F-5 that entered service as the Hellcat

Hellcat Mk I

Most of the Hellcat's service took place over the Pacific, but this 800 squadron example in full invasion stripes was operating off HMS *Emperor*, covering Operation Dragoon, the landings in southern France during August 1944.

II. By August 1945, 10 squadrons were operating the Hellcat, including examples of both the reconnaissance and night-fighting versions. The latter forming the equipment of the final two British Hellcat unit, disbanded in August 1946. Total production of this spectacularly successful fighter, which continued for a mere three years and one month, was 12,275.

Grumman Hellcat Mk.I

Weight: (Maximum takeoff) 6000kg (13217lbs)
Dimensions: Length: 10.17m (33ft 4in), Wingspan: 13.08m (42ft 10in), Height: 4.4m (14ft 5in)
Powerplant: One 149kW (2000hp) Pratt & Whitney R-2800-10 Double Wasp two row 18-cylinder air-cooled radial piston engine
Speed: 600km/h (373mph)
Range: 1755km (1090 miles)
Ceiling: 11,438m (37,500ft)
Crew: 1
Armament: Six 12.7mm (0.5in) Browning AN/M2 machine guns fixed forward-firing in wings; up to 907kg (2000lb) bombload

Grumman Hellcat Mk.II

The Royal Navy received a total of 1263 Hellcats over the course of the war. This example was serving with 804 Squadron aboard HMS *Ameer* as part of the British East Indies Fleet engaged in operations over Sumatra and Malaya in 1945.

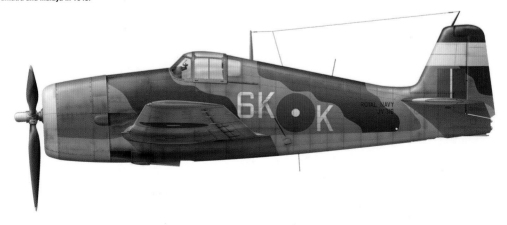

Grumman F6F-5P Hellcat, VF-84, USS *Bunker Hill*, 1945

The F6F-5P was a reconnaissance variant (the P standing for 'Photo') carrying camera equipment in the rear fuselage. Despite this, the F6F-5P retained the same armament capability as a standard fighter Hellcat. This aircraft is depicted as it appeared as the Hellcats of VF-84 supported the invasion of Iwo Jima.

Wing and tail structure
In stark contrast to its Japanese foes, the Hellcat was immensely strong. The three spar wing, although of conventional construction, was the largest by area fitted to any single-engine wartime fighter, and in contrast to the Wildcat was designed to be folded from the start.

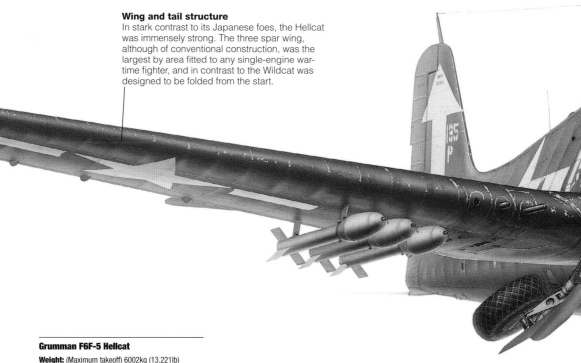

Grumman F6F-5 Hellcat
Weight: (Maximum takeoff) 6002kg (13,221lb)
Dimensions: Length: 10.17m (33ft 4in), Wingspan: 13.08m (42ft 10in), Height: 4.4m (14ft 5in)
Powerplant: One 149kW (2000hp) Pratt & Whitney R-2800-10 Double Wasp two row 18-cylinder air-cooled radial piston engine
Speed: 600km/h (373mph)
Range: 2606km (1620 miles) with external fuel tank
Ceiling: 11,438m (37,500ft)
Crew: 1
Armament: Six 12.7mm (0.5in) Browning AN/M2 machine guns fixed forward-firing in wings

Cockpit

The F6F-3 and -5 resemble each other very closely but the -5 had the fuselage windows immediately aft of the cockpit hood blanked off. The -5 also features simplified framing around the windscreen with an integral bulletproof section allowing for an improved forward view.

Armament

With the exception of a handful of cannon-eqipped F6F-5N night fighters, the Hellcat's gun armament of six 12.7mm (0.5in) machine guns remained unchanged for the duration of its production. The F6F-5 could also carry a variety of stores, including the 127mm (5in) rockets depicted here.

External stores

Range capability was a major factor for all naval fighters and the Hellcat was no exception. External tanks could be fitted on both the centreline and underwing hardpoints. The range of the F6F-5 with external fuel tanks was an impressive 2460km (1,530 miles).

F6F-5 Hellcat

Cutaway key
1 Radio mast
2 Rudder balance
3 Rudder upper hinge
4 Aluminium alloy fin ribs
5 Rudder post
6 Rudder structure
7 Rudder trim tab
8 Rudder middle hinge
9 Diagonal stiffeners
10 Aluminium alloy elevator trim tab
11 Fabric-covered (and taped) elevator surfaces
12 Elevator balance
13 Flush-riveted leading-edge strip
14 Arrestor hook (extended)
15 Tailplane ribs
16 Tail navigation (running) light
17 Rudder lower hinge
18 Arrestor hook (stowed)
19 Fin main spar lower cut-out
20 Tailplane end rib
21 Fin forward spar
22 Fuselage/finroot fairing
23 Port elevator
24 Aluminium alloy-skinned tailplane
25 Section light
26 Fuselage aft frame
27 Control access
28 Bulkhead
29 Tailwheel hydraulic shock-absorber
30 Tailwheel centring mechanism
31 Tailwheel steel mounting arm
32 Rearward-retracting tailwheel (hard rubber tyre)
33 Fairing
34 Steel plate door fairing
35 Tricing sling support tube
36 Hydraulic actuating cylinder
37 Flanged ring fuselage frames
38 Control cable runs
39 Fuselage longerons
40 Relay box
41 Dorsal rod antenna
42 Dorsal recognition light
43 Radio aerial
44 Radio mast
45 Aerial lead-in
46 Dorsal frame stiffeners
47 Junction box
48 Radio equipment (upper rack)
49 Radio shelf
50 Control cable runs
51 Transverse brace
52 Remote radio compass
53 Ventral recognition lights (three)
54 Ventral rod antenna
55 Destructor device
56 Accumulator
57 Radio equipment (lower rack)
58 Entry hand/footholds
59 Engine water injection tank
60 Canopy track
61 Water filler neck
62 Rear-view window
63 Rearward-sliding cockpit canopy (open)
64 Headrest
65 Pilot's head/shoulder armour
66 Canopy sill (reinforced)
67 Fire extinguisher
68 Oxygen bottle (port fuselage wall)

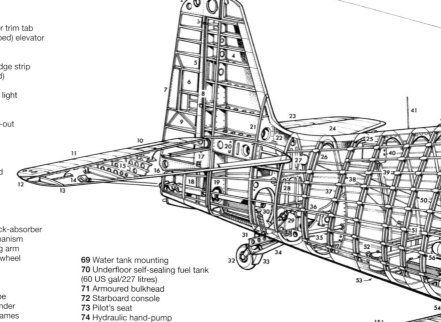

69 Water tank mounting
70 Underfloor self-sealing fuel tank (60 US gal/227 litres)
71 Armoured bulkhead
72 Starboard console
73 Pilot's seat
74 Hydraulic hand-pump
75 Fuel filler cap and neck
76 Rudder pedals
77 Central console
78 Control column
79 Chart board (horizontal stowage)
80 Instrument panel
81 Panel coaming
82 Reflector gunsight
83 Rear-view mirror
84 Armoured glass windshield
85 Deflection plate (pilot forward protection)
86 Main bulkhead (armour-plated upper section with hoisting sling attachments port and starboard)
87 Aluminium alloy aileron trim tab
88 Fabric-covered (and taped) aileron surfaces
89 Flush-riveted outer wing skin
90 Aluminium alloy sheet wingtip (riveted to wing outer rib)
91 Port navigation (running) light
92 Formed leading edge (approach/landing light and camera gun inboard)
93 Fixed cowling panel
94 Armour plate (oil tank forward protection)
95 Oil tank (19 US gal/ 72 litres)
96 Welded engine mount fittings
97 Fuselage forward bulkhead
98 Aileron control linkage

99 Engine accessories bay
100 Engine mounting frame (hydraulic fluid reservoir attached to port frames)
101 Controllable cooling gills
102 Cowling ring (removable servicing/access panels)
103 Pratt & Whitney R-2800-10W twin-row radial air-cooled engine
104 Nose ring profile
105 Reduction gear housing
106 Three-bladed Hamilton Standard Hydromatic controllable-pitch propeller
107 Propeller hub
108 Engine oil cooler (centre) and supercharger intercooler

109 Oil cooler deflection plate under-protection
110 Oil cooler duct
111 Intercooler intake duct
112 Mainwheel fairing
113 Port mainwheel
114 Auxiliary tank support/attachment arms
115 Cooler outlet and fairing
116 Exhaust cluster
117 Supercharger housing
118 Exhaust outlet scoop
119 Wing front spar web
120 Wing front spar/fuselage attachment bolts
121 Undercarriage mounting/pivot point on front spar
122 Inter-spar self-sealing fuel tanks (port and starboard: 87.5 US gal (133 litres) each)
123 Wing rear spar/fuselage attachment bolts
124 Structural end rib
125 Slotted wing flap profile
126 Wing flap centre section
127 Wing fold line
128 Starboard wheel well (doubler-plate reinforced edges)
129 Gun bay
130 Removable diagonal brace strut
131 Three 0.5-in (12.7-mm) Colt Browning machineguns

139 Auxiliary tank sling/brace
140 Long-range auxiliary fuel tank (jettisonable)
141 Mainwheel aluminium alloy fairing
142 Forged steel torque link
143 Low pressure balloon tyre
144 Cast magnesium wheel
145 Underwing 5-in (12.7-cm) air-to-ground RPS
146 Mark V zero-length rocket launcher installation
147 Canted wing front spar
148 Inter-spar ammunition box bay (lower surface access)
149 Wing rear spar (normal to plane of wing)
150 Rear sub spar
151 Wing flap outersection
152 Frise-type aileron
153 Aileron balance tab

132 Auxiliary tank aft support
133 Blast tubes
134 Folding wing joint (upper surface)
135 Machine-gun barrels
136 Fairing
137 Undercarriage actuating strut
138 Mainwheel leg oleo hydraulic shock strut

154 Wing outer rib
155 Wing lateral stiffeners
156 Aileron spar
157 Wing outer-section ribs
158 Leading-edge rib cut-outs
159 Starboard navigation (running) light
160 Pitot head
161 Underwing stores pylon (mounted on fixed centre-section inboard of mainwheel leg)
162 Auxiliary fuel tank

Grumman F7F Tigercat

One of very few twin-piston engine planes designed from the outset as a carrier aircraft, the potent Tigercat demonstrated exceptional performance and saw the briefest of wartime service.

Grumman had developed and flown the twin-engine XF5F Skyrocket fighter during 1940 but despite showing considerable promise, the pressures of war resulted in its cancellation, allowing the company to concentrate on development of the more conventional Hellcat. Both the US Navy and Grumman had remained interested in the large twin-engine fighter and with the design of the huge new Midway-class carriers under way, development of a more powerful version of the same concept was initiated.

Slim fuselage

First flown in December 1943, the F7F was the first aircraft with a nose wheel undercarriage ordered by the US Navy. A shoulder-wing aircraft with large underslung nacelles for its two R-2800 engines, the fuselage – intended to present as small a frontal area as possible to minimize drag – was notably slim. Armament was four machine guns in the nose and four 20mm (0.79in) cannons in the wing roots. Performance was excellent but trials demonstrated operating the Tigercat from a carrier

Grumman F7F-2N Tigercat

Despite having missed any meaningful service in World War II, the Tigercat was utilized quite extensively in Korea. This F7F-3N was on the strength of HEDRON-1 (1st Marine Aircraft Wing Headquarters Squadron) at Pohang, Korea, in 1952.

deck was difficult and the decision was taken to equip 12 Marine Corps squadrons with the F7F.

Only 35 of the initial F7F-1 single-seat model were built before production switched to the F7F-2N, a two-seat night-fighter featuring a cockpit for a radar operator behind the pilot and an AN/APS-6 radar unit replacing the nose guns. The first Marine Corps unit to convert to the F7F-2N, VMF(N)-533, arrived on Okinawa on 14 August 1945, the day before the Japanese surrender, subsequently flying operational patrols in the area before moving to China.

Production of the Tigercat continued post-war with 250 of the improved single-seat F7F-3 variant, of which 60 were converted to F7F-3N night fighters. Both of these variants would see combat in Korea before all Tigercats were withdrawn in 1952.

Grumman F7F-1 Tigercat

Weight: (maximum takeoff) 10,730kg (23,636lb)

Dimensions: Length: 13.85m (45ft 5in), Wingspan: 15.7m (51ft 6in), Height: 5.06m (16ft 7in)

Powerplant: Two kW (2100hp) Pratt & Whitney R-2800-22W CDouble Wasp 18-cylinder air-cooled radial engines

Speed: 687km/h (427mph)

Range: 1882km (1170 miles), 2880km (1790 miles) with 1136 (300 gallon) litre external tank

Ceiling: 11,040m (36,200ft)

Crew: 1

Armament: Four AN/M3 20mm (0.79in) cannon in wing roots, four 12.7mm (0.5in) M2 Browning machine guns in fuselage nose; up to two 454kg (1000lb) bombs or eight 12.7mm (0.5in) rockets under wings, one 1136 litre (300 US gallon) fuel tank or one 568 litre (150 US gallon) napalm tank under fuselage

---

Ryan FR-1 Fireball

Ryan's Fireball was the only fighter equipped with both a piston and jet engine to enter service.

Despite the huge performance potential of the jet engine, early jet powered aircraft required long take-off runs, possessed high landing speeds and consumed fuel at a prohibitive rate, all qualities that were impractical for a carrier fighter. It was therefore proposed by the US Navy to utilize a conventional piston-engined aircraft fitted with a turbojet in the tail to act as a supplementary power unit. The piston engine would confer good take-off and landing characteristics while offering an acceptable range and the jet could be utilized to boost speed and climb performance when necessary.

A requirement for such an aircraft was issued in December 1942 and Ryan responded quickly with the XFR-1 that flew for the first time on 25 June 1944. Fitted with a Wright Cyclone in the nose and a General Electric I-16 jet engine buried in the rear fuselage, the only clue to its radical power plant were the large wing root air intakes and the tricycle undercarriage adopted to avoid the jet engine scorching the deck – a serious consideration at the time as US carriers featured wooden decks. Development proceeded quickly and an order for

100 FR-1s was placed on 2 December 1943, later increased to 700 aircraft.

Production model

Production FR-1s appeared in March 1945 and began to form the equipment of VF-66, a unit created specifically to bring the Fireball into service. However, during the spring of 1945, two accidents, one fatal, caused the loss of the third prototype and an early production machine prompting a major investigation and delaying service entry. After some structural strengthening and the imposition of a maximum load factor of 5g rather than the 7.5g as designed, the Fireball completed its carrier qualification trials during May. VF-66 were preparing for deployment in the Pacific when the war came to an abrupt end on 15 August 1945 and production of the FR-1 was terminated at the 66th aircraft. Ryan produced a prototype of a more advanced version featuring a General Electric XT31-GE-2 turboprop in the nose and J31 jet engine the fuselage, which flew in 1946 but no production ensued. Meanwhile the FR-1 remained in service until mid-1947.

Ryan FR-1 Fireball

With the exception of its exotic jet powerplant, the Fireball was a relatively conventional aircraft for its era. This example was flying with VF-1E (as VF-66 had been redesignated) in mid 1947 aboard USS *Badoeng Strait* as denoted by the BS tail code.

Ryan FR-1 Fireball

Weight: (Maximum takeoff) 4810kg (10,595lb)

Dimensions: Length: 9.86m (32ft 4in), Wingspan: 12.2m (40ft), Height: 3.97m (13ft)

Powerplant: One 1063kW (1425hp) Wright R-1820-72W Cyclone nine-cylinder air-cooled radial engine

Speed: 685km/h (426mph)

Range: 1657km (1030 miles)

Ceiling: 13,145m (43100ft)

Crew: 1

Armament: Four 12.7mm (0.5in) Browning MG 53-2 machine guns; up to eight 12.7mm (0.5in) rockets underwing and one 454kg (1000lb) bomb under fuselage

---

Grumman F8F Bearcat

The ultimate extrapolation of Grumman's wartime fighter development, the Bearcat was the most potent American piston-engine fighter ever to operate from a carrier deck.

Grumman F8F-1 Bearcat

The orange rear fuselage band of this Bearcat signifies that it is serving with a unit of the US Naval Air Reserve, in this case VF-882 based at Olathe Naval air station in Kansas in 1948. With the appearance of higher performance jet fighters, the Bearcat was withdrawn from US service in 1952.

In 1943, with the F6F Hellcat successfully established in production, Grumman began the development of a higher performance aircraft to replace it. During June 1942 Jake Swirbul, the vice president of Grumman, met with F4F Wildcat pilots who had fought at the Battle of Midway to canvas their opinions about what they wanted from a carrier fighter and it became clear that they regarded rate of climb as among the most important attributes of any new fighter.

With no US engine available possessing greater power than the R-2800 of the Hellcat, the only way to achieve a significant improvement in climb performance was to design the smallest and lightest possible airframe around the existing engine and the F8F as first flown in August 1944 was 1.5m (5ft) shorter than the Hellcat and 2.1m (7ft) shorter in span. It also proved to be 80km/h (50mph) faster than the F6F and demonstrated a spectacular rate of climb – in 1946 a standard Bearcat would set a time-to-

height record of 3028m (10,000ft) in 94 seconds, a record that would stand for 10 years.

End of war

Orders for over 2000 of the new aircraft were placed and deliveries began in February 1945, with the first unit VF-19 receiving its aircraft in May. This unit was enroute to the Pacific theatre aboard USS *Langley* when the conflict came to a close and as such saw no action.

By this time Grumman had built just over 200 F8Fs and post-war production would see 765 built in total. Post-war the Bearcat was for a time the most numerous fighters in US Navy service, equipping 28 squadrons by mid-1949. However, by 1951 all had been replaced by jets in frontline units.

Grumman F8F-1 Bearcat

Weight: (Maximum takeoff) 5878kg (12,947lb)

Dimensions: Length: 8.62m (28ft 3in), Wingspan: 10.94m (35ft 10in), Height: 4.23m (13ft 10in)

Powerplant: One kW (2,100hp) Pratt & Whitney R-2800-34W CDouble Wasp 18-cylinder air-cooled radial engine

Speed: 677km/h (421mph)

Range: 1778km (1105 miles), 3162km (1965 miles) with external tanks

Ceiling: 11,804m (38,700ft)

Crew: 1

Armament: Four 12.7mm (0.5in) M2 Browning machine guns in wings; up to two 454kg (1000lb) bombs or four 12.7mm (0.5in) rockets under wings

McDonnell FH-1 Phantom

The US Navy's first pure jet aircraft, the FH-1 Phantom was also the first jet powered aircraft intended to be operated from a carrier, the first naval aircraft to exceed 805km/h (500mph) and the first production aircraft of the McDonnell company.

McDonnell FH-1 Phantom

This FH-1 was operating with VF-171 aboard USS *Midway* during 1949. VF-171 (then designated VF-17A) had become the first fully operational US jet carrier unit when it deployed aboard USS *Saipan* in May 1948.

The McDonnell Aircraft company only came into existence in 1938 but Navy officials were impressed by their experimental XP-67 'Moonbat' fighter and asked the company to tender a submission in a competition to design the Navy's first jet fighter. Their winning design, two prototypes of which were ordered in August 1943, was intended to be powered by no fewer than six 136kg (300lb) thrust axial flow jet engines of 24cm (9.5in) diameter mounted side by side in the wing roots.

Twin-engined design

This was found to impose too high a wing loading for carrier operations and McDonnell settled instead on a twin-engine design after studies showed this arrangement to be lighter and possess simpler design, control and instrumentation. The Westinghouse 19XB engine, subsequently to be designated the J30, was selected as

the power unit but, as was usually the case with early jet aircraft, engine development lagged considerably behind airframe production.

As a consequence, when the first XFD-1 prototype was ready to begin testing only one engine had been cleared for flight and on 26 January 1945 the first flight of the new jet fighter was made with a single engine, ballast replacing the second.

Prototype testing

A contract for 100 FD-1s was placed on 7 March 1945 but the end of the war saw this reduced to 60. Halfway through the production run the designation changed to FH-1 (the letter 'D' having been reassigned to Douglas) by which time the second prototype had become the first American pure jet aircraft to operate from a carrier when it performed a series of takeoff and landings on USS *Franklin D. Roosevelt* on 21 July 1946.

McDonnell FH-1 Phantom
Weight: (maximum takeoff) 4327kg (9531lb)
Dimensions: Length: 11.36m (37ft 3in), Wingspan: 12.43m (40ft 9in), Height: 4.3m (14ft 9in)
Powerplant: Two 726kg (1600lb) static thrust Westinghouse WE-19XB-28 (J30) axial-flow turbojets
Speed: 777km/h (483mph)
Range: 1206km (750 miles)
Ceiling: 13,328m (43,700ft)
Crew: 1
Armament: Four 12.7mm (0.5in) M2 Browning machine guns in fuselage nose

The Phantom's time in frontline units would be short as more capable jet fighters were quickly developed, but it served as a training aircraft until 1954.

Hawker Sea Fury

Developed in the closing months of World War II, the Sea Fury was the final piston-engine fighter design to enter British service and was to prove highly successful.

The naval variant of the Fury represented the ultimate development of the line of Hawker fighters that began with the Typhoon in early 1940. The Fury had been developed as a lightened version of the Hawker Tempest, in part influenced by the example of the Focke Wulf Fw 190 after Hawker engineers studied a captured example in mid-1942. Although the Fury would be tested with the Rolls-Royce Griffon and Napier Sabre, it was the Bristol Centaurus that powered the first example to fly on 1 September 1944 and the same engine was also selected for the navalized version, which was flown for the first time on 21 February 1945, although the definitive second prototype with five-bladed propeller and folding wings only flew in October.

Engine failure

Testing revealed that the Centaurus engine was prone to crankshaft failures due to an inadequate lubrication system. This was solved by a switch to the improved Bristol Centaurus 18,

Hawker Sea Fury FB.11

WE790 was on the strength of the Royal Australian Navy during the Korean War. Sea Furies operated from the Australian carrier HMAS *Sydney* and Australia would operate the type until 1960.

although not before several early Sea Furies had suffered in-flight engine seizures. The initial production version, the F Mk X, entered service in February 1947 and the Sea Fury would ultimately equip 30 British units with 615 of the 864 built serving with the Royal Navy, mostly of the FB Mk.11 version optimized for the fighter-bomber role. The Sea Fury saw action in the Korean war, famously scoring a 'kill' against a MiG-15 jet fighter and was only retired from Royal Naval Volunteer Reserve units in 1955. The aircraft enjoyed considerable success on the export market, serving with 10 other air arms and became one of comparatively few fighters to have scored victories for both sides during the Cold War when Cuban Sea Furies downed two CIA B-26s during the Bay of Pigs invasion attempt of 1961.

Hawker Sea Fury FB Mk.11

Weight: (Maximum takeoff) 6645kg (14,650lb)

Dimensions: Length: 10.57m (34ft 8in), Wingspan: 11.7m (38ft 5in), Height: 4.84m (15ft 11in)

Powerplant: One 1850kW (2,480hp) Bristol Centaurus 18-cylinder air-cooled radial engine

Speed: 740km/h (460mph)

Range: 1260km (780 miles)

Ceiling: 10,900 m (35,800ft)

Crew: 1

Armament: Four fixed forward firing 20mm (0.79in) Hispano Mk V cannon; up to 910kg (2000lb) of bombs or 16 7.62mm (3in) rockets under wings

de Havilland Sea Hornet

Designed for an island-hopping campaign in the Pacific, the supremely elegant de Havilland Sea Hornet was one of the fastest piston-engine fighters ever built.

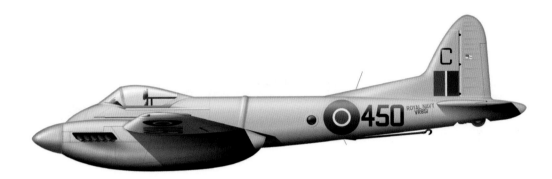

Initial development of the Hornet envisioned it as essentially a scaled-down Mosquito optimized for high-altitude operations. Talks between the Ministry of Aircraft Production and de Havilland resulted in the design being modified as a general purpose fighter with particular emphasis placed on range capability. With exceptional performance being forecast for the new fighter, the Air Ministry wrote specification F.12/43 around it and the prototype, by now named Hornet, flew on 28 July 1944.

Naval interest in the Hornet was high from early in the development process and the construction of a navalized version followed swiftly after the standard landplane. The Sea Hornet featured folding wings and an arrestor hook, which added a weight penalty of 249kg (550lb) – but its performance was still outstanding.

The first Sea Hornet flew on 19 April 1945 with carrier trials commencing in August aboard HMS *Ocean*. An initial batch of 64 Sea Hornet F. Mk 20s was ordered but

the end of the war meant they would serve with only one operational unit, 806 squadron, aboard the carriers HMS *Implacable* and *Indomitable*.

Superb handling

In service the Sea Hornet proved popular due to its amazing performance and beautiful handling, Royal Navy pilots finding it to be a good match for the RAF's jet-powered Gloster Meteor fighter in mock-combat. The aircraft would also be developed into a night fighter, the NF.Mk 21, 78 of which were constructed. The night fighter was instantly recognizable by its long and slender nose radome, housing an ASH radar set, the operator for which was seated under a small bubble canopy level with the wing's trailing edge. The NF.Mk 21 would also only serve with one unit, 809 squadron, which went to sea aboard HMS *Vengeance*.

Despite the small numbers built, Sea Hornets persisted in service for over a decade, at least two remaining on Royal Navy strength in 1957.

de Havilland Sea Hornet F.20

VR851 was one of three 806 squadron Royal Navy Sea Hornets embarked on HMCS *Magnificent* for a North American tour in 1948. The Sea Hornets performed flying displays at the New York International Air Exposition during July and early August of that year.

De Havilland Sea Hornet F.Mk 20

Weight: (Maximum takeoff) 9117kg (20,100lb)

Dimensions Length: 11.2m (36ft in), Wingspan: 13.7m (45ft)

Powerplant: Two 1544kW (2070hp) Rolls-Royce Merlin 130 (port) and 131 (starboard) V-12 liquid-cooled piston engines

Speed: 748km/h (465mph)

Range: 3113km (1934 miles) with external tanks

Ceiling: 11,185m (36,700ft)

Crew: 1

Armament: Four 20mm (0.79in) Hispano cannon fixed firing forward in lower forward fuselage; up to 2000lb bombload or eight 27kg (60lb) rockets underwing

BOMBERS & TORPEDO BOMBERS

The only sufficiently accurate methods for aircraft to sink ships in the late 1930s were by dive bombing or torpedo attack and, accordingly, aircraft tended to be optimized for one or other mission. As the war progressed, both types of aircraft were increasingly used to attack onshore targets and a more general strike aircraft, epitomized by the underpowered Barracuda in the UK and the superlative Skyraider in the US, paved the way for post-war development.

This chapter includes the following aircraft:

- Blackburn Shark
- Fairey Swordfish
- Douglas TBD Devastator
- Curtiss SBC Helldiver
- Vought SB2U Vindicator
- Blackburn Skua
- Loire-Nieuport LN.401
- Fairey Albacore
- Douglas SBD Dauntless
- North American B-25B
- Fairey Barracuda
- Curtiss SB2C Helldiver
- Brewster SB2A Buccaneer
- Grumman TBF Avenger
- de Havilland Sea Mosquito
- Martin AM-1 Mauler
- Douglas AD-1 Skyraider

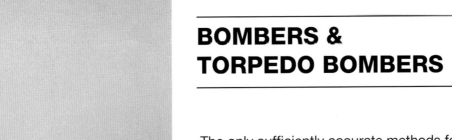

Arguably the UK's most important naval aircraft, the Swordfish's archaic appearance belied the profound usefulness of this versatile, rugged machine.

Blackburn Shark

The Blackburn Shark was a contemporary of the Fairey Swordfish and, in some regards, a superior aircraft. However, an unfortunate choice of engine effectively condemned the Shark to obscurity.

Blackburn had supplied several successful carrier-based torpedo bombers to the Fleet Air Arm – indeed they had been the sole supplier of this type of aircraft from 1921 to 1936 and the Shark, which first flew on 24 August 1933, was a sound design that was widely expected to emulate the success experienced by its progenitors. It featured Warren truss wing bracing that virtually eliminated flying wires, a watertight metal monocoque fuselage of great strength and in later examples an enclosed cockpit. It possessed excellent flying characteristics, being virtually impossible to stall, and could carry a heavy load.

However, although Blackburn wanted the Bristol Pegasus to power the Shark, the Air Ministry insisted that they utilize the Armstrong-Siddeley Tiger VI instead. This engine was unreliable and prone to severe vibration that resulted in oil pipes severing, leading to engine seizure as well as metal fatigue in the engine mounts.

Blackburn Shark Mk.I

In many ways a superior aircraft to the Fairey Swordfish, the failure to develop the Shark remains something of a mystery. This example was serving with 820 Squadron aboard HMS *Courageous* in 1937 during the Shark's brief service as a frontline carrier aircraft.

Although Blackburn worked hard to eradicate the problems and largely succeeded, the Fairey Swordfish was available by 1937 and the Air Ministry ordered that aircraft instead, relegating the Sharks to target tugging duties.

Limited combat role

Meanwhile the RCAF had ordered the type and specified that it should be fitted with the Pegasus engine Blackburn had wanted all along. Two RCAF Sharks were supplied by Blackburn and a further 17 were built by Boeing Canada and delivered reliable service in the coastal patrol role until 1944. The Shark saw combat only on two occasions: one of the Canadian

Blackburn Shark Mk.II

Weight: (Maximum takeoff) 3679kg (8111lb)
Dimensions: Length: 10.74m (35ft 3in), Wingspan: 14m (456ft), Height: 3.68m (12ft 1in)
Powerplant: One 570kW (760hp) Armstrong-Siddeley Tiger VI 14-cylinder air-cooled radial piston engine
Speed: 240km/h (150mph)
Range: 1006km (625 miles)
Ceiling: 4800m (15,600ft)
Crew: 3
Armament: One 7.7mm (0.303in) Vickers machine gun fixed forward firing in nose, one 7.7mm (0.303in) Vickers K machine gun flexibly mounted in dorsal position; up to 730kg (1600lb) bombload or one 460mm (18in) torpedo

aircraft surprised a German U-boat on the surface off the Canadian coast and attacked it with bombs, although with uncertain results. Then, during December 1941, an RAF Shark target tug based at Seletar in Singapore was hastily fitted with bomb carriers to attack the advancing Japanese forces.

Fairey Swordfish

Painfully slow and seemingly outdated even when it entered service, the Swordfish nonetheless sank a greater tonnage of Axis shipping than any other Allied aircraft and served for the duration of the conflict.

Resembling a relic from World War I and with a performance to match, it is quite amazing that the Fairey Swordfish was able to accomplish so much during World War II.

The whole programme got off to a bad start when the immediate forerunner to the Swordfish, the prototype Fairey TSR I (standing for Torpedo Spotter Reconnaissance), designed originally for a Greek Air Force requirement, was lost when it entered an unrecoverable spin on 11 September 1933, although the pilot managed to escape by parachute.

At the same time as the TSR I Fairey were also working on a liquid-cooled Rolls-Royce Kestrel powered fleet-spotter reconnaissance aircraft to Air Ministry specification S.9/30, which was incomplete at the time of the TSR I's accident.

After the loss of the TSR I Fairey elected to modify the design and submit it for the updated specification S.15/33 calling for a Naval carrier-borne torpedo bomber/spotter/reconnaissance aircraft.

New design

Fairey redesigned the aircraft with a differently shaped vertical tail, extended fuselage and slightly swept back wings to eliminate the irrecoverable spin problem and the new TSR II took its maiden flight on 17 April 1934. The prototype was submitted for service flight testing at Martlesham Heath aerodrome, while later in the year float-equipped TSR IIs were tested for catapult launches and recovery at sea on the battlecruiser HMS *Repulse*.

Trials proved successful and the first batch of 86 TSR IIs was ordered in April 1935, and the name Swordfish Mk I was bestowed on the aircraft around the same time. The Swordfish was typical of British naval aircraft designs of the financially squeezed 1920s and 30s in that it sought to combine several, somewhat incompatible, roles in one airframe and, on the power of its 510kW (690hp) Bristol Pegasus IIIM3, was profoundly unambitious in performance, being a mere 42km/h

Fairey Swordfish Mk.I

Pictured as it appeared when it entered service, this Swordfish was on the strength of 823 Squadron aboard HMS *Victorious* in 1936. The horizontal fin stripes denote that this is the CO's aircraft.

Fairey Swordfish I

Weight: (Maximum takeoff) 4196kg (9250lb)

Dimensions: Length: 10.87m (35ft 8in), Wingspan: 13.87m (45ft 6in), Height: 3.76m (12ft 4in)

Powerplant: One 510kW (690hp) Bristol Pegasus 30 9-cylinder air-cooled radial piston engine

Speed: 224km/h (139mph)

Range: 840km (522 miles)

Ceiling: 5000m (16500ft)

Crew: 3

Armament: One fixed forward-firing 7.7mm (0.303in) Browning machine gun in upper fuselage nose, one 7.7mm (0.303in) Vickers K gun flexibly mounted in rear cockpit; one 730kg (1670lb) torpedo, up to 700kg (1500lb) bombload

(26mph) faster than the Sopwith Cuckoo torpedo bomber of 1918 and 107km/h (67mph) slower than

Fairey Swordfish I

Weight: (Maximum takeoff) 4196kg (9250lb)

Dimensions: Length: 10.87m (35ft 8in), Wingspan: 13.87m (45ft 6in), Height: 3.76m (12ft 4in)

Powerplant: One 510kW (690hp) Bristol Pegasus 30 9-cylinder air-cooled radial piston engine

Speed: 224km/h (139mph)

Range: 840km (522 miles)

Ceiling: 5000m (16500ft)

Crew: 3

Armament: One fixed forward-firing 7.7mm (0.303in) Browning machine gun in upper fuselage nose, one 7.7mm (0.303in) Vickers K gun flexibly mounted in rear cockpit; one 730kg (1670lb) torpedo, up to 700kg (1500lb) bombload

its monoplane contemporary, the American Douglas TBD.

Versatile performance

The Swordfish I entered service aboard the carrier HMS *Glorious* with 825 Squadron in July 1936, initially replacing the Fairey Seal spotter-reconnaissance aircraft but later the Blackburn Baffin torpedo bomber as well. The aircraft gained a further degree of versatility during 1939 when successful trials were undertaken to assess its suitability for dive bombing. Production built up rapidly, such that the Fleet Air Arm could boast 13 operational squadrons on the outbreak of war. In addition, floatplane Swordfish equipped three Flights whose aircraft were distributed among

Fairey Swordfish Mk.I

Likely the Swordfish's most famous action, the attack on the *Bismarck* was flown in terrible weather conditions and played a critical part in the sinking of the pocket battleship. K8375 of 810 Squadron was one of the aircraft that performed the attack from HMS *Ark Royal* on 26 May 1941.

Fairey Swordfish Mk.I

The floatplane Swordfish was an important aircraft in its own right and achieved some notable 'firsts', not least sinking the first U-boat lost to aircraft in WWII. This example was aboard HMS *Malaya* during 1940.

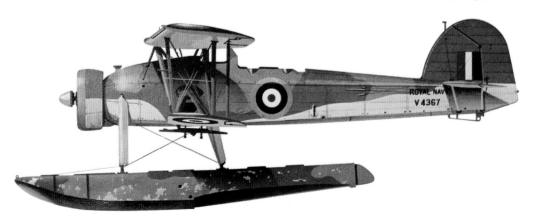

catapult equipped capital ships. Early war operations saw the Swordfish attain a number of firsts. At Trondheim in Norway, Swordfish attacked two destroyers on 11 April 1940, scoring a hit on one of them, in the first torpedo attack of the war by aircraft. Later in the same month a Swordfish floatplane operating from battleship HMS *Warspite* dived-bombed and sank the German submarine U-64, the first enemy submarine sunk by an aircraft in World War II. The same Swordfish

had earlier flown in the spotter role and radioed gunnery corrections during the second battle of Narvik during which eight German destroyers were sunk or scuttled without British loss.

Attack on Taranto

Arguably the zenith of the Swordfish's combat career occurred in November of that year with the spectacular Taranto raid in which half of Italy's Mediterranean fleet was knocked out by 21 Swordfish while in harbour.

However, the Swordfish's most famous action was in May 1941 when aircraft flying from *Ark Royal*, in appalling weather, attacked the German battleship *Bismarck,* disabling her rudder and rendering her unable to escape her pursuers, which directly led to her sinking.

Significantly, during that action the Swordfish had flown so slowly that *Bismarck*'s fire predictors had been unable to cope and her anti-aircraft shells exploded prematurely. In

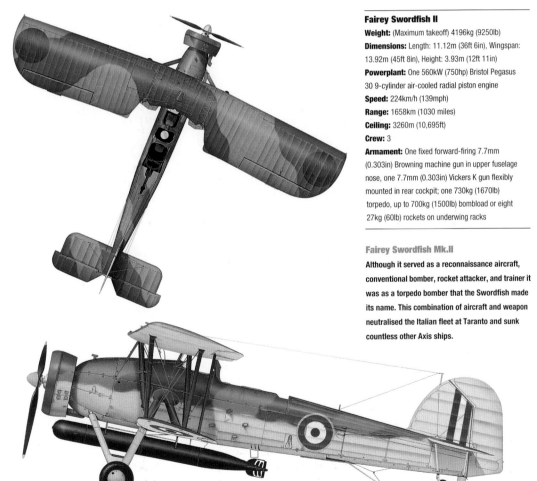

Fairey Swordfish II
Weight: (Maximum takeoff) 4196kg (9250lb)
Dimensions: Length: 11.12m (36ft 6in), Wingspan: 13.92m (45ft 8in), Height: 3.93m (12ft 11in)
Powerplant: One 560kW (750hp) Bristol Pegasus 30 9-cylinder air-cooled radial piston engine
Speed: 224km/h (139mph)
Range: 1658km (1030 miles)
Ceiling: 3260m (10,695ft)
Crew: 3
Armament: One fixed forward-firing 7.7mm (0.303in) Browning machine gun in upper fuselage nose, one 7.7mm (0.303in) Vickers K gun flexibly mounted in rear cockpit; one 730kg (1670lb) torpedo, up to 700kg (1500lb) bombload or eight 27kg (60lb) rockets on underwing racks

Fairey Swordfish Mk.II
Although it served as a reconnaissance aircraft, conventional bomber, rocket attacker, and trainer it was as a torpedo bomber that the Swordfish made its name. This combination of aircraft and weapon neutralised the Italian fleet at Taranto and sunk countless other Axis ships.

Fairey Swordfish Mk.III
Operating from land in the spring of 1945 with 119 Squadron RAF of Coastal Command, this radar-equipped Swordfish III was utilised for nocturnal anti-shipping and submarine patrols over the North Sea. The longevity of the Swordfish, outdated when it was introduced, was remarkable.

addition, much of her flak was unable to fire on the Swordfish at all, as they had flown so low that the guns could not depress sufficiently to hit them.

New Mk II

Production of the Mk.I gave way to the Mk.II, deliveries of which began in November 1941. By now it was clear that the Swordfish could not expect to survive if enemy fighters were present and the Swordfish's extremely docile deck landing characteristics and exceptional short take off performance saw it increasingly utilized on escort carriers as an anti-submarine warfare asset, a role in which it was unlikely to meet enemy aircraft and in which it excelled. The Mk.II featured a slightly more powerful Pegasus 30 engine and metal-skinned lower wings. The latter allowed the aircraft to carry and fire rockets as its primary mission moved away from torpedo attack and increasingly encompassed other roles. On 23 May 1943, an aircraft of 819 squadron sank a U-boat in the

first successful rocket projectile attack delivered by a Swordfish. Over the course of the war Swordfish would account for 22 submarines sunk, including four in a single voyage by aircraft operating from HMS *Vindex* during September 1944 while escorting a convoy through the Arctic sea. The Mk.II would be the most produced Swordfish variant, with 1080 built all by Blackburn under sub-contract.

Rocket Assisted Take Off Gear

The Mk.III, all of which were built by Blackburn, was the final version and was identical to the Mk.II save for the addition of a large fairing between the undercarriage legs containing ASV Mk X radar that was capable of detecting a surface vessel at a range of 40km (25 miles); it could even detect the *schnorkel* engine intake of a submerged U-boat in calm conditions, although at a much reduced range. The addition of a draggy and heavy radar in addition to the myriad different weapons the Swordfish could carry, with no concomitant increase in engine power, saw the Swordfish struggle to get airborne and necessitated the use of Rocket Assisted Take Off Gear (RATOG) that could spectacularly throw the biplane into the air a mere 82m (269ft) after rocket ignition. The radar equipment now allowed the Mk.III to

Fairey Swordfish III

Weight: (Maximum takeoff) 4196kg (9250lb)
Dimensions: Length: 10.87m (35ft 8in), Wingspan: 13.87m (45ft 6in), Height: 3.76m (12ft 4in)
Powerplant: One 560kW (750hp) Bristol Pegasus 30 9-cylinder air-cooled radial piston engine
Speed: 222km/h (138mph)
Range: 1658km (1030 miles)
Ceiling: 5000m (16500ft)
Crew: 3
Armament: One fixed forward-firing 7.7mm (0.303in) Browning machine gun in upper fuselage nose, one 7.7mm (0.303in) Vickers K gun flexibly mounted in rear cockpit; one 730kg (1670lb) torpedo, up to 700kg (1500lb) bombload or eight 27kg (60lb) rockets on underwing racks

operate in the anti-shipping role at night and black painted examples flew in RAF hands from Bircham Newton on the east coast of England to attack German E-boats and S-Boats before switching their attention to midget submarines sailing from Holland, three confirmed sinkings of which were

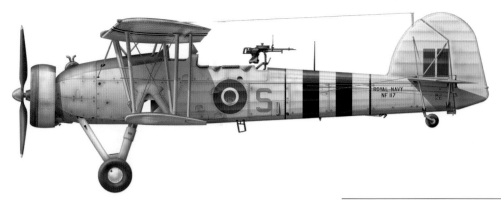

Fairey Swordfish Mk.II
With full D-Day stripes on the fuselage and wings, this Swordfish was serving with 811 Squadron aboard HMS *Biter*. At the time of the Normandy landings Biter was engaged in convoy escort work, carrying rocket-armed Swordfish IIs.

achieved until the final sorties were made on 8 May 1945 (VE Day). The last operational Swordfish of all were flown by the Fleet Air Arm's composite unit 836 squadron that comprised 91 aircraft which served aboard various Merchant Aircraft Carriers (MAC ships) as anti-submarine escorts. This unit stood down on 21 May 1945.

As well as British-based units, the Swordfish also served with the RAAF in Australia and RCAF in

Canada. The latter service adoped an enclosed cockpit on both Mk.IIs and Mk.IIIs to deal with the very low temperatures of the Canadian winter. This enclosed cockpit version is sometimes referred to as the Mk.IV but this is a retrospective designation and was not used at the time. In total, 2391 Swordfish were built, 1699 by Blackburn (often referred to as 'Blackfish') and this slow but easy to fly and profoundly reliable aircraft inspired a remarkable level of affection in its crews.

Throughout its career the Swordfish was known by the homely nickname of 'Stringbag' in reference to its ability, like the then ubiquitous string bag used for shopping, to carry more or less anything.

Fairey Swordfish II
Weight: (Maximum takeoff) 4196kg (9250lb)
Dimensions: Length: 11.12m (36ft 6in), Wingspan: 13.92m (45ft 8in), Height: 3.93m (12ft 11in)
Powerplant: One 560kW (750hp) Bristol Pegasus 30 9-cylinder air-cooled radial piston engine
Speed: 224km/h (139mph)
Range: 1658km (1030 miles)
Ceiling: 3260m (10,695ft)
Crew: 3
Armament: One fixed forward-firing 7.7mm (0.303in) Browning machine gun in upper fuselage nose, one 7.7mm (0.303in) Vickers K gun flexibly mounted in rear cockpit; one 730kg (1670lb) torpedo, up to 700kg (1500lb) bombload or eight 27kg (60lb) rockets on underwing racks

Fairey Swordfish Mk.I
The Swordfish of 821 Squadron, including P4210, were aboard HMS *Ark Royal* during 1940, and supported operations in the Norwegian campaign.

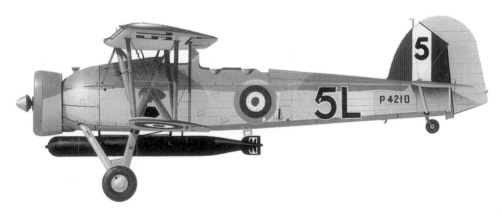

Swordfish Mk.II

Cutaway key

1 Rudder structure
2 Rudder upper hinge
3 Diagonal brace
4 External bracing wires
5 Rudder hinge
6 Elevator control horn
7 Tail navigation light
8 Elevator structure
9 Fixed tab
10 Elevator balance
11 Elevator hinge
12 Starboard Tailplane
13 Tailplane struts
14 Lashing down shackle
15 Trestling foot
16 Rear wedge
17 Rudder lower hinge
18 Tailplane adjustment screw
19 Elevator control cable
20 External bracing wires
21 Elevator fixed tab
22 Tailfin structure
23 Bracing wire attachment
24 Aerial stub
25 Bracing wires
26 Port elevator
27 Port Tailplane
28 Tailplane support struts
29 Dinghy external release cord
30 Tailwheel oleo shock absorber
31 Non-retractable Dunlop tailwheel
32 Fuselage framework
33 Arrestor hook housing
34 Control cable fairleads
35 Dorsal decking
36 Rod aerial
37 Lewis gun stowage trough
38 Aerial
39 Flexible 7.7mm (0.303in) Lewis machine gun
40 Fairey high-speed flexible gun mounting
41 Type O-3 compass mounting points
42 Aft cockpit coaming
43 Aft cockpit
44 Lewis drum magazine stowage
45 Radio installation
46 Ballast weights
47 Arrestor hook pivot
48 Fuselage lower longeron
49 Arrestor hook
(part extended)
50 Aileron hinge
51 Fixed tab
52 Starboard upper aileron
53 Rear spar
54 Wing ribs
55 Starboard formation light
56 Starboard navigation light
57 Aileron connect strut
58 Interplane struts
59 Bracing wires
60 Starboard lower aileron
61 Aileron hinge
62 Aileron balance
63 Rear spar
64 Wing ribs
65 Aileron outer hinge
66 Deckhandling/ lashing grips
67 Front spar
68 Interplane strut attachments
69 Wing internal diagonal bracing wires
70 Flying wires
71 Wing skinning

72 Additional support wire (fitted when underwing stores carried)
73 Wing fold hinge
74 Inboard interplane struts
75 Stub plane end rib
76 Wing locking handle
77 Stub plane structure
78 Intake slot
79 Side window
80 Catapult spool
81 Drag struts
82 Cockpit sloping floor

83 Fixed 7.7mm (0.303in) Vickers gun (deleted from some aircraft)
84 Case ejection chute
85 Access panel
86 Camera mounting bracket
87 Sliding bomb-aiming hatch
88 Zip inspection flap
89 Fuselage upper longeron
90 Centre cockpit
91 Inter-cockpit fairing
92 Upper wing aerial mast
93 Pilot's headrest
94 Pilot's seat and harness
95 Bulkhead
96 Vickers gun fairing

97 Fuel gravity tank (12.5 Imp gal/ 57 litre capacity)
98 Windscreen
99 Handholds
100 Flap control handwheel and rocking head assembly
101 Wing centre section
102 Dinghy release cord handle
103 Identification light
104 Centre section pyramid strut attachment

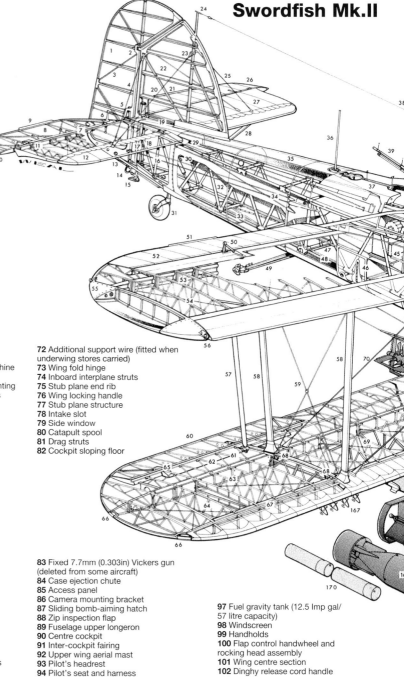

105 Diagonal strengtheners
106 Dinghy inflation cylinder
107 Type C dinghy stowage well
108 Aileron control linkage
109 Trailing edge rib sections
110 Rear spar
111 Wing rib stations
112 Aileron connect strut
113 Port upper aileron
114 Fixed tab
115 Aileron hinge
116 Port formation light
117 Wing skinning
118 Port navigation light
119 Leading-edge slot

131 Four 27kg (60lb) anti-shipping rocket projectiles
132 Three-blade fixed-pitch Fairey-Reed metal propeller
133 Spinner
134 Townend ring

148 Vickers gun trough
149 Fuselage forward frame
150 Oil cooler
151 Fuel filter
152 Stub plane/fuselage attachment

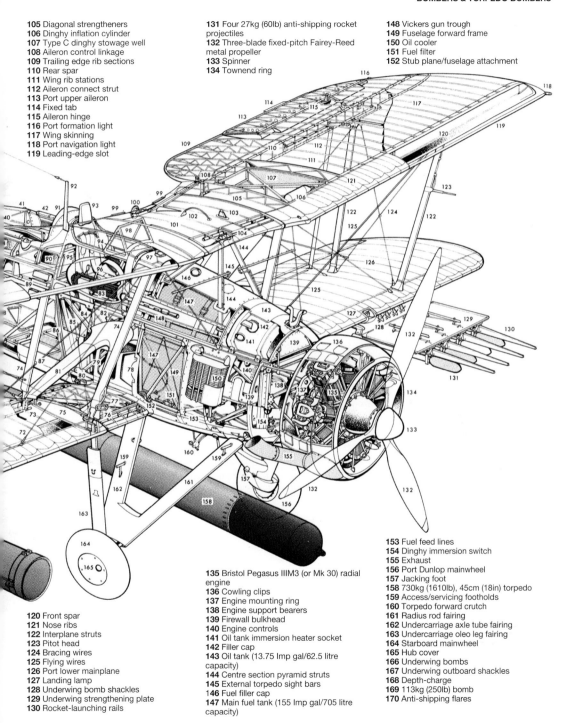

135 Bristol Pegasus IIIM3 (or Mk 30) radial engine
136 Cowling clips
137 Engine mounting ring
138 Engine support bearers
139 Firewall bulkhead
140 Engine controls
141 Oil tank immersion heater socket
142 Filler cap
143 Oil tank (13.75 Imp gal/62.5 litre capacity)
144 Centre section pyramid struts
145 External torpedo sight bars
146 Fuel filler cap
147 Main fuel tank (155 Imp gal/705 litre capacity)

120 Front spar
121 Nose ribs
122 Interplane struts
123 Pitot head
124 Bracing wires
125 Flying wires
126 Port lower mainplane
127 Landing lamp
128 Underwing bomb shackles
129 Underwing strengthening plate
130 Rocket-launching rails

153 Fuel feed lines
154 Dinghy immersion switch
155 Exhaust
156 Port Dunlop mainwheel
157 Jacking foot
158 730kg (1610lb), 45cm (18in) torpedo
159 Access/servicing footholds
160 Torpedo forward crutch
161 Radius rod fairing
162 Undercarriage axle tube fairing
163 Undercarriage oleo leg fairing
164 Starboard mainwheel
165 Hub cover
166 Underwing bombs
167 Underwing outboard shackles
168 Depth-charge
169 113kg (250lb) bomb
170 Anti-shipping flares

Douglas TBD Devastator

Painfully illustrating the pace of aviation development in the late 1930s, the Douglas TBD Devastator was considered one of the most advanced carrier aircraft in the world when it entered service in 1937, but once committed to action in early 1942 it proved to be outdated and vulnerable.

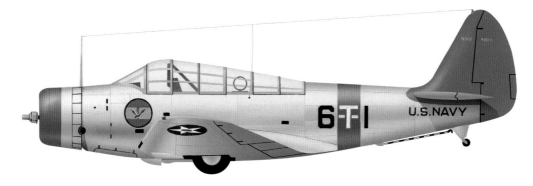

First flown on 15 April 1935, the XTBD-1 was one of the winners of a competition to supply the USN with new bombing aircraft. It was simultaneously the US Navy's first mass-produced carrier-based monoplane, its first with a fully enclosed cockpit and hydraulically folding wings, and that service's first all-metal aircraft. Intended to be able to perform torpedo and conventional bombing attacks, the aircraft was fitted with a Norden bombsight for level bombing, the bombardier utilizing this from a prone position under the pilot and aiming through a window just behind the engine cowling. When not in use this window was covered by clamshell doors. The undercarriage was semi-retractable – when raised the wheels protruded about 25cm (10in) below the lower surface of the wing - and was intended to minimize damage in the event of a wheels-up landing.

Acceptance trials

The XTBD-1 was reliable, easy to fly and thanks to its generous wing area and large flaps possessed a landing speed of merely 95km/h (59mph), rendering it simple to deck land. It sailed through acceptance trials during 1935 and only relatively minor changes were made for the production TBD-1, most noticeably a taller canopy allowing for the inclusion of a rollover bar. On 3 February, 110 TBD-1s were ordered, which at that time was the largest aircraft order placed by the US Navy during peacetime. Production would eventually total 129 as further airframes were ordered in August 1938 to replace those lost in training.

Carrier qualification and torpedo trials were undertaken as the aircraft entered production, continuing into 1937, and the first examples were delivered to frontline units in October of that year beginning with VT-3 aboard USS *Saratoga*. The TBD went on to serve aboard all five of the carriers the USN was operating in late 1937.

By December 1941, the TBD – by now named the Devastator – was already slated for replacement by the Grumman TBF, but none had been delivered by the time of Pearl Harbor.

Douglas TBD-1 Devastator

Pictured as it appeared when new in typically colourful prewar USN markings, this TBD-1 served with VT-6 (the same unit as the aircraft on the opposite page) and wears the squadron's white albatross insignia under the windscreen. This unit operated TBDs from 1938 until shortly after the Battle of Midway in 1942.

Douglas TBD-1

Weight: (Maximum takeoff) 4624kg (10194lb)

Dimensions: Length: 10.67m (35ft), Wingspan: 15.24m (50ft), Height: 4.6m (15ft 1in)

Powerplant: One 670kW (900hp) Pratt & Whitney R-1830-64 Twin Wasp 14-cylinder air-cooled radial piston engine

Speed: 332km/h (206mph)

Range: 1152km (715 miles)

Ceiling: 5900m (19,500ft)

Crew: 3

Armament: One 7.62mm (0.30in) Browning M1919 machine gun fixed forward firing in cowling, one 7.62mm (0.30in) Browning M1919 machine gun flexibly mounted in rear cockpit; up to 453kg (1000lb) bombload or one 907kg (2000lb) Mk XIII torpedo

Initially the TBD proved effective, damaging the carrier *Shokaku* and sinking the carrier *Shoho* in concert with SBDs at the Battle of the Coral Sea. However, the June 1942 Battle of Midway exposed the shocking vulnerability of the TBD and the appalling unreliability of the Mark XIII torpedo. Of 41 aircraft committed, only six came back (although one of these was forced to ditch due to lack of fuel) and not a single torpedo struck its target. After Midway, remaining TBDs were quickly withdrawn in favour of TBFs and transferred to training and other second-line units. The final example, used by the 'Commander,

Fleet Air Activities, West Coast', was withdrawn in November 1944.

Interest was also expressed in a floatplane version of the TBD and accordingly in August 1939 the first production example was modified with a pair of EDO floats, allegedly the largest ever fitted to a single-engine aircraft, and designated the TBD-1A. The Netherlands were interested in employing the aircraft as a coastal patrol floatplane but unfortunately the German invasion of May 1940 ended any prospect of a Dutch sale. With no order forthcoming from the US Navy or any other buyer the TBD-1A remained a one-off. However, it performed

important service in development work on the unreliable Mark XIII torpedo.

The TBD-1A's slow speed and stable handling proved ideal for performing these tests, resulting in a number of improvements to the Mark.XIII, and it served for six years as a testbed before being retired in September 1943, arguably contributing more to the war effort than its unfortunate carrier-based brethren.

A Douglas TBD-1 Devastator drops a Mark XIII torpedo during exercises in the Pacific, 20 October 1941. This plane is aircraft number 6-T-10, from Torpedo Squadron Six (VT-6), based on USS *Enterprise* (CV-6).

Curtiss SBC Helldiver

The final frontline combat biplane in US service, the SBC Helldiver was the last of a distinguished line of Curtiss carrier biplanes. Surprisingly, the design originally flew as a monoplane.

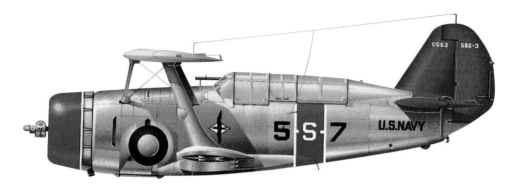

The Helldiver started life as the Curtiss Model 73, a two-seat parasol monoplane carrier fighter with a folding wing. Rejected for the fighter role, the aircraft was proposed as a scout bomber but the parasol wing failed during dive-bombing tests, although the pilot was able to land the damaged machine. In response Curtiss proposed reworking the aircraft as a biplane, the second lower wing adding strength to the design although at the expense of the wing folding ability. The Navy agreed and the resulting SBC proved satisfactory, prompting the USN to order 83 production examples that began to appear in 1937. A further 124 of the improved SBC-4 were ordered in January 1938.

Frontline service

During 1938 the SBC-3 went to sea with three of the five USN scouting squadrons aboard USS *Enterprise*, *Saratoga* and *Yorktown* although only the USS *Lexington* ever operated the SBC-4. The pace of aviation

Curtiss SBC-3 Helldiver

Pictured as it appeared in 1937, the red tail surfaces of this Helldiver of VS-5 signify that the aircraft was serving aboard USS *Yorktown*. The blue engine cowling and fuselage band indicate this was the leader of the squadron's 3rd section, while the unit badge below the windscreen depicts a frigatebird in flight.

development was such that all the SBCs had been replaced by the SBD Dauntless on carriers before the US entered the war in December 1941. The Helldiver subsequently enjoyed much useful service as a training aircraft, the last being withdrawn in October 1944. Meanwhile, flying with the Marine Corps in Samoa the SBC persisted in frontline service in the scouting role until June 1943, although it never saw combat.

In early 1940, 90 SBCs were ordered by the French *Aeronavale* and were aboard the carrier *Bearn* in the Atlantic when France capitulated. *Bearn* subsequently diverted to Martinique where the SBCs, among other aircraft, were offloaded. Stored in the open,

Curtiss SBC-4

Weight: (Maximum takeoff) 33,462kg (7632lb)
Dimensions: Length: 8.58m (28ft 2in), Wingspan: 10.36m (34ft), Height: 3.18m (10ft 5in)
Powerplant: One 630kW (850hp) Wright R-1820-34 Cyclone 9-cylinder air cooled radial piston engine
Speed: 377km/h (234mph)
Range: 652km (405 miles)
Ceiling: 7300m (24,000ft)
Crew: 2
Armament: One 7.6mm (0.3in) M1919 Browning machine gun fixed forward-firing in nose, one 7.6mm (0.3in) M1919 Browning machine gun flexibly mounted in rear cockpit; up to 454kg (1000lb) bombload

the tropical conditions ravaged the structure of the SBCs that never flew again and were scrapped during 1942. Five of the French SBCs were never loaded onto *Bearn* and were instead utilized by the RAF who named the aircraft the Cleveland I, using them for communications and ground instruction.

Vought SB2U Vindicator

The first monoplane dive bomber in US Navy service, the SB2U Vindicator was still in use with Marine Corps units in 1943 and saw combat at the Battle of Midway as well as in French hands during the Battle for France.

During the mid-1930s the US Navy was sufficiently anxious about the ability of monoplanes to operate from carriers that it issued a specification for both a monoplane and a biplane to fill its requirement for a new carrier scout bomber. Vought built a prototype in both categories, the XSB2U-1 monoplane and biplane XSB3U-1. The biplane unsurprisingly demonstrated an inferior performance and was not proceeded with. However, the XSB2U-1 that flew on 4 January 1936 was ordered into production as the SB2U-1 Vindicator, of which 56 were built, with a further 58 ordered of the slightly modified SB2U-2. A more substantial change resulted in the SB2U-3, which was intended primarily for Marine Corps use and designed to utilize either wheels or floats interchangeably. Featuring an increased fuel capacity for greater range, the SB2U-3s would be the only variant in US service to see combat during the war.

Serving aboard USS *Ranger* with VS-41 in August 1941, immediately before the aircraft's withdrawal from frontline operations, this SB2U-1 was engaged in scouting missions over the Atlantic.

French use

The Vindicator also attracted the attention of the French *Aeronavale,* who would be the first to take the aircraft into action. The French operated the Vought V-156-F, an export model equivalent to the US SB2U-2 but featuring several items of French equipment and instrumentation. Despite training on the carrier *Bearn,* the V-156s would operate solely from land bases when war broke out, the carrier being considered too slow and vulnerable for operational use. Flown by *escadrilles* AB1 and AB3, the V-156s were utilized in a series of attacks on bridges and German positions, sustaining heavy losses in the process. After contributing to the air cover over

Vought SB2U-3 Vindicator

Weight: (Maximum takeoff) 4273kg (9421lb)

Dimensions: Length: 10.36m (34ft), Wingspan: 12.77m (41ft 11in), Height: 4.34m (14ft 3in)

Powerplant: One 615kW (825hp) Pratt & Whitney R-1535-02 Twin Wasp Junior 14-cylinder air-cooled radial piston engine

Speed: 391km/h (243mph)

Range: 1800km (1120 miles)

Ceiling: 7200m (23,600ft)

Crew: 2

Armament: One 12.7mm (0.5in) M2 Browning machine gun in starboard wing, one 12.7mm (0.5in) M2 Browning machine gun flexibly mounted in rear cockpit; up to 453kg (1000lb) bombload under fuselage

the Dunkirk evacuation beaches the two Vought units moved south to fight the Italians and are believed to have sunk an Italian submarine off Albenga, north-western Italy. After the fall of France, 50 further V-156s on French order were taken over for Royal Naval use and named the Chesapeake I by the British.

The Chesapeake featured several improvements specified by the Royal Navy, including additional armour and heavier forward firing armament, along with the larger fuel tanks of the SB2U-3. Intended for anti-submarine patrol work, the first Chesapeake unit, 811 squadron, formed on 14 July 1941 to go aboard the escort carrier HMS *Archer*. Unfortunately, testing revealed that the aircraft were too underpowered to carry a meaningful payload, so the Fairey Swordfish was used by 811 squadron instead and the Chesapeake was reassigned to training units.

Battle of Midway

In the US, the Vindicator had been replaced by the Dauntless on carriers by December 1941 but continued to be used by the US Navy as a training aircraft. Few Marine Corps units ever operated the SB2U and one of these, VMSB-231 consisting of both SB2U-3s

and SBD-2 Dauntlesses, was formed on Midway Island on 1 March 1942 to defend the island in the event of a Japanese attack.

During the subsequent Battle of Midway the squadron lost 23 out of 30 aircraft over the course of 4–6 June. During this action, Captain Richard E. Fleming was posthumously awarded the Medal of Honor for continuing his attack on the Japanese cruiser *Mikuma*

A Vought SB2U-1 Vindicator takes off from USS *Saratoga* (CV-3), 8 February 1938.

despite the fact his SB2U had been hit and set on fire. When VMSB-231 left Midway during September 1943 they left behind three SB2U-3s that were, by then, the last three Vindicators in US service anywhere.

Vought V-156-F

This aircraft was assigned to *Escadrille* 10 of AB3 at Cuers in July 1940. Attrition of the French V-156s was high, the aircraft proving vulnerable to enemy fighters and ground fire. At the armistice, only eight aircraft survived of 40 originally ordered by the *Aeronavale*.

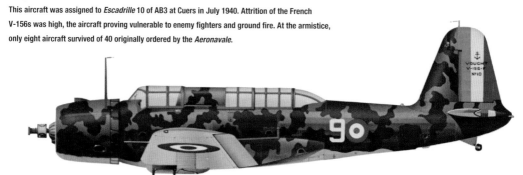

Blackburn Skua

The first monoplane to serve with the Fleet Air Arm, the Skua was intended to fulfil the roles of both dive bomber and fighter. Although withdrawn from frontline use during 1941, the Skua was the first aircraft in history to sink an enemy capital ship during wartime.

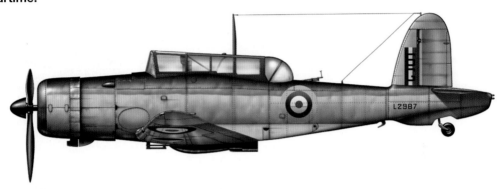

During 1934, discussions between the Air Ministry and the Royal Navy resulted in specification O.27/34 being issued calling for a dive bomber that could also function as a fighter. The Admiralty believed that a pilot could not navigate with sufficient accuracy on his own at sea and thus the aircraft was compelled to be a two-seater, but it was considered unlikely that the aircraft would ever meet land-based fighters and thus the modest performance of such an aircraft relative to a single-seat fighter was believed to be an acceptable concession, a design philosophy that would later compromise the performance of both the Fairey Fulmar and Firefly.

Blackburn's response to O.27/34 was judged the best and 150 production machines were ordered in March 1936 along with two prototypes, the first of which flew on 9 February 1937. Stability problems resulted in the aircraft's nose being lengthened 73cm (2ft 5in) and the horizontal tail surfaces were also extended. The aircraft also proved reluctant to recover from a spin and as an interim measure an anti-spin

parachute was fitted in the extreme tail, this 'interim' feature subsequently appearing on all production Skuas as the spinning issues were never entirely resolved. Wing dihedral was found to be too shallow, resulting in further instability. Rather than redesign the entire wing, which would have delayed production, Blackburn fitted the Skua with distinctive upturned wingtips that had much the same effect but did not require any major engineering changes. When the aircraft was subsequently developed into the Roc turret fighter, the opportunity was taken for a more thorough redesign and the Roc discarded the upturned wingtips.

Test flights

In this form the aircraft went into production as the Skua Mk.II, the prototype thus becoming the sole Mk I. 800 squadron were the first unit to receive the Skua II in late 1938, taking the aircraft to sea aboard HMS *Ark Royal* in the spring of 1939 for an intense period of service test flying during which the Skua was generally found to be easy to fly, with pleasant

Blackburn Skua Mk.II

Expected to operate as a dive bomber and a fighter, the Skua proved effective at the former but mediocre at best at the latter. L2987 was on the strength of 800 Squadron in June 1940 aboard HMS *Ark Royal* in the Mediterranean, and was lost when it ran out of fuel escorting Hurricanes to Malta.

Blackburn Skua Mk.II

Weight: (Maximum takeoff) 3732kg (8228lb)
Dimensions: Length: 10.85m (35ft 7in), Wingspan: 14.07m (46ft 2in), Height: 3.81m (12ft 6in)
Powerplant: One 660kW (890hp) Bristol Perseus XII 9-cylinder, air-cooled, radial piston engine
Speed: 362km/h (225mph)
Range: 1220km (760 miles)
Ceiling: 6200m (20,200ft)
Crew: 2
Armament: Four 7.7mm (0.303in) Browning machine gun fixed forward-firing in wings, one 7.7mm (0.303in) Vickers K or Lewis machine gun flexibly mounted in rear cockpit; up to 227kg (500lb) bombload

handling and a good deck landing aircraft. During this period, dive bombing techniques were developed, with the aircraft proving to be an excellent platform for this form of attack using its patented Zap flaps as dive brakes.

By the outbreak of war three squadrons were flying Skuas and they would be in action within a fortnight, though the first combat use of the Skua was little more than an embarrassment: of three Skuas attacking submarine U-30, two were forced to ditch after being damaged by their own bombs and their crews rescued, to become prisoners of war, by the very U-boat they were attacking. Matters improved on 26 September 1939 when Skuas intercepted and shot down a Dornier Do 18 flying boat, the first confirmed British air-to-air victory of the war. Despite the Skua's generally underwhelming performance as a fighter, the first Royal Navy 'ace' of the war was Skua pilot William Lucy, who scored all five of his confirmed victories in the aircraft.

Finest moment

The Skua's finest moment came in April 1940 when it achieved a genuine milestone, becoming simultaneously the first aircraft to sink a major enemy warship in wartime and the first aircraft to sink a ship by dive bombing. A total of 16 Skuas, led by the aforementioned William Lucy, flew from RAF Hatston in the Orkney Islands and dive bombed and sank the cruiser *Königsberg* at anchor in Bergen harbour. Further dive-bombing attacks were made as part of the Norwegian campaign and heavy losses were incurred during a raid on the battleship *Scharnhorst* in Trondheim.

Operations covering the Dunkirk beaches and in the Mediterranean were fairly successful against Axis bomber aircraft but it was becoming increasingly clear that the Skua could not hold its own against enemy fighters and the aircraft was gradually withdrawn from frontline use with the final unit, 801 squadron, relinquishing its Skuas in May to reform on Sea Hurricanes in August. The fact that the Skua had proved an excellent dive bomber wasn't enough to

make up for its vulnerability as a fighter and effectively deprived the Fleet Air Arm of an effective dive bomber for the next three years until the Barracuda entered service.

Second-line roles

The Skua had been designed with potential second-line duties in mind and subsequently operated as a target tug, with both the Navy and the RAF, serving in many more second-line units than it ever had operationally. Its reliable Perseus engine, coupled with the immensely strong airframe and good handling, made the aircraft eminently suitable for the target tug role, although even here its low speed left something to be desired. The Skua nearly remained in service for the duration of the conflict, but not quite – the final Skua tug in service was struck off charge in March 1945.

Blackburn Skua Mk. IIs of 803 Squadron in formation over the southern English coast, 1939.

Loire-Nieuport LN.401

The only French-designed carrier aircraft to see combat during World War II, the Loire-Nieuport LN.401 was available in only trivial numbers and saw brief but very intense action.

The LN.401 consisted of an aerodynamically cleaned-up version of the earlier LN.140, a two-seat naval dive-bomber that had failed to win a production contract. The LN.40 project dispensed with the second crewman and added retractable undercarriage in place of the fixed units of the earlier aircraft. The first prototype LN.40 flew on 6 July 1938 followed by several pre-production aircraft during 1939 and the aircraft passed its carrier trials aboard *Bearn*. During tests it was found that the dive brakes fitted on the rear fuselage were ineffective and that extending undercarriage doors worked far more satisfactorily.

A further 36 production aircraft were ordered in early 1939 as the LN.401, with a further 36 LN.411s, identical except for the removal of naval equipment, ordered for the *Armee de l'Air*. In the event, these aircraft were rejected as too slow and passed to the Navy, who operated both variants.

During the invasion of France the LN401 and 411s were used to attack advancing German ground forces and found to be seriously vulnerable.

Loire-Nieuport LN.401

The LN.401 proved terribly vulnerable when committed to action. This aircraft from *Escadrille* AB2 belly-landed after being hit by flak during an attack on the bridge over the Sambre a l'Oise canal and the pilot was captured.

On one raid on 19 May 1940 of 20 Loire-Nieuports committed, 10 were shot down and a further seven so badly damaged that they were written off. Surviving aircraft were transferred to the south of France to fight the Italians.

LN.402 upgrade

During the war an improved version with a more powerful Hispano-Suiza engine was flown as the LN.402 in November 1939 but none were produced before France capitulated. A more radical development that ditched the Stuka-like inverted gull wing and distinctive tailplane fins to produce an altogether cleaner looking airframe was completed shortly before the fall of France. Designated the LN.42, it was successfully hidden from the Germans until the end of the war and flight tested in August 1945 by which time it was totally outdated.

Loire-Nieuport LN.401

Weight: (Maximum takeoff) 2835kg (6250lb)
Dimensions: Length: 9.75m (32ft), Wingspan: 14m (45ft 11in), Height: 3.5m (11ft 6in)
Powerplant: One 510kW (690hp) Hispano-Suiza 12Xcrs V-12 liquid-cooled piston engine
Speed: 299km/h (186mph)
Range: 1200km (750 miles)
Ceiling: 9500m (31,200ft)
Crew: 1
Armament: One 20mm Hispano cannon and two four 7.5mm (0.295in) Darne machine guns fixed forward-firing in wings; up to 225kg (496lb) bombload

Fairey Albacore

Intended to replace the Swordfish on British carriers, the Albacore never entirely supplanted its famous forebear but nonetheless saw much intense action, proving effective in a number of demanding roles and theatres.

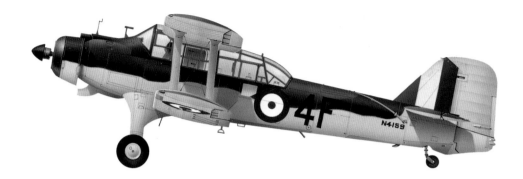

With the Swordfish established in production during 1936, attention switched to its replacement that was intended to fulfil all the functions of the Swordfish and be easily convertible into a floatplane. From the start the Admiralty required that the crew were to be housed in an enclosed, heated cockpit but it was unclear at first whether the new aircraft would be a monoplane or biplane. Fairey, although they favoured the monoplane, prepared no less than 17 different designs of both biplane and monoplane configuration featuring different engine types.

In the end the Admiralty favoured a Bristol Taurus-powered biplane machine stating that their decision was "dictated principally by the requirements of take-off, the limitation dimensions and mechanical difficulties in wing folding": in other words, doubts were still harboured that a monoplane could possess sufficient strength and lift to operate successfully from a carrier.

First flight

Construction was held up by the Taurus engine programme falling behind schedule and the first prototype only performed its first flight on 12 December 1938, despite the first order for 100 production aircraft having been placed as early as May 1937. As well as the fully enclosed crew accommodation, a great leap forward in comfort when compared to the open-cockpit Swordfish, the Albacore featured the sleeve-valve two-row Taurus engine, which was not only a very smooth-running and quiet engine but also delivered more power than the Pegasus fitted to the Swordfish. The propeller was a constant speed unit from the start and the airframe featured an innovative all-metal monocoque fuselage that possessed inherent buoyancy, a boon in the event of ditching at sea. Furthermore, the Albacore possessed an automatic system for deploying the life raft if a forced landing was made on water.

Fairey Albacore Mk.I

826 Squadron flew the Albacore from March 1940 to August 1943. This aircraft is depicted as it appeared when 826 Sqdn was embarked upon HMS *Formidable* for convoy escort duty in the winter of 1940-41. The unit was later shore-based in the Western Desert.

Fairey Albacore Mk.I

Weight: (Maximum takeoff) 5820kg (12,830lb)

Dimensions: Length: 12.13m (39ft 10in), Wingspan: 15.24m (50ft), Height: 4.65m (15ft 3in)

Powerplant: One 794kW (1065hp) Bristol Taurus II or one 840kW (1130hp) Bristol Taurus XII 14-cylinder, air-cooled, radial piston engine

Speed: 272km/h (169mph)

Range: 1497km (930 miles)

Ceiling: 6309m (20,700ft)

Crew: 2 or 3

Armament: One 7.7mm (0.303in) Browning machine gun fixed forward-firing in starboard wing, one or two 7.7mm (0.303in) Vickers K machine guns flexibly mounted in rear cockpit; up to 907kg (2000lb) bombload or one 730kg (1610lb) torpedo

---

Poor reliability

Testing revealed few problems, poor stalling characteristics were cured before the aircraft entered service by moving the centre of gravity further aft and the Albacore proved generally pleasant to fly with a superb view for the pilot and good deck landing characteristics. Unfortunately, when tested as a floatplane, the Albacore was found to be susceptible to severe porpoising, even in calm conditions, with water being thrown up onto the engine and propeller, and as a result the decision was made to drop the floatplane requirement.

Initial deliveries to units began in December 1939 and the Albacore's operational use commenced during March 1940, although early service use was plagued by reliability issues affecting the Taurus engine, which were bad enough to result in all Albacores being grounded for a month during the summer of 1940. The problems were largely ironed out but an unfortunate reputation for poor reliability would nonetheless dog the Taurus for the remainder of its service life.

First combat use of the Albacore fell to 826 squadron, initially a shore-based Royal Navy unit, covering the evacuation from Dunkirk before coming under RAF Coastal Command control and being used as a dive-bombing unit to attack shore targets and German shipping, performing convoy escort duties and dropping mines when not required for bombing missions.

By the end of November 1940, 826 squadron also became one of the first two units, along with 829 squadron, to take the Albacore to sea, embarking on HMS *Formidable* for convoy escort duty down the West African coast before transferring to the Mediterranean where the Albacores of these two units would prove decisive during the Battle of Cape Matapan. During this action many torpedo attacks were launched, damaging the Italian battleship *Vittorio Veneto* and disabling the cruiser *Pola* that directly led to its destruction, along with two other cruisers rendering assistance, by British surface vessels. Albacores were subsequently kept busy in actions ranging from the Kirkenes and Petsamo raids in Norway to fighting Japanese forces in Malaya. Albacores made the only torpedo attack on

the *Tirpitz* at sea, attacked Vichy French airfields as part of Operation Torch, and flew intense nocturnal operations in the Western Desert, dive bombing enemy positions by night and illuminating targets for RAF heavy bombers with flares.

From late 1941 until the summer of 1943 Albacores played a significant role in the defence of Malta, seeing relentless action attacking Axis shipping, mostly at night to avoid enemy fighters, and were kept in the air only through the Herculean efforts of groundcrew in a theatre where spares and equipment were extremely limited. By the end of 1943 the aircraft was generally being replaced by the monoplane Barracuda in most roles but persisted in limited frontline use into 1945.

Radar-guided attacks

Oddly for a Naval aircraft, the final unit to operate the Albacore was 119 Squadron RAF, a Coastal Command unit that utilized the aircraft to make radar-guided attacks on E-boats by night. This squadron divested itself of its last Albacores in March 1945, replacing them, somewhat ironically, with the Fairey Swordfish, the very aircraft the Albacore had been designed to supersede. Production of the Albacore totalled 800, plus three prototypes, all of which had been ordered before the war broke out. Only one variant was ever produced but there were many detail differences between airframes.

Douglas SBD Dauntless

One of the few truly decisive combat aircraft in history, the SBD Dauntless – despite its borderline obsolescence, slow speed and apparent vulnerability – enjoyed a spectacularly successful career.

Oddly, the aircraft that would become the Douglas SBD began life as the Northrop BT-1, a dive bomber first flown on 19 August 1935. Although 54 BT-1s were built, serving on both USS *Yorktown* and *Enterprise*, the aircraft was not considered a success, proving to have problematic low speed handling characteristics, which was a serious problem for a carrier aircraft. Despite its less than stellar deck landing capability, one BT-1 was fitted with a fixed tricycle undercarriage as the BT-1S to test the suitability of such an undercarriage for carrier use. It became the first tricycle gear aircraft to land on a carrier in the process, although after being damaged on 6 February 1939 this aircraft was altered back to standard BT-1 configuration.

Northrop began work on an improved version called the BT-2, which differed externally most obviously from its progenitor in replacing the large fairings into which the undercarriage (partially) retracted rearwards with a neater inward-retracting landing gear that fully enclosed the wheels and gear legs in the wing. The prototype

XBT-2 also featured an engine change, the R-1535 Twin Wasp Junior of the BT-1 being replaced by a Wright 1820 Cyclone of similar power. By the time the XBT-2 flew on 25 April 1938 Northrop had been taken over by the Douglas Aircraft Company to become the Douglas El Segundo division, as a result the Northrop XBT-2 became the Douglas XSBD and orders were placed for both the SBD-1 for the Marine Corps and SBD-2, featuring increased fuel capacity, for the Navy.

Diving characteristics

In contrast to the BT-1, the new SBD handled well and was easy to deck land. It was manoeuvrable and its distinctive perforated dive brakes were effective, conferring excellent diving characteristics upon the aircraft. The SBD possessed a long range, but by world standards the aircraft was not very fast, crews joking that the SBD designation stood for 'Slow But Deadly'. Nonetheless this did not stop the SBD being utilized, due to a shortage of single-seat fighters, for combat air patrols around US fleets,

Douglas SBD-1 Dauntless

VMB-1, based at Quantico, Virginia, was the second Marine Corps unit to receive SBDs, taking delivery of their new aircraft in late 1940. The initial SBD-1 variant was a rare aircraft, only 57 were built.

Douglas SBD-1

Weight: (Maximum take-off) 4441kg (9790lb)
Dimensions: Length: 9.78m (32ft 1in), Wingspan: 12.66m (41ft 6in), Height: 4.14m (13ft 7in)
Powerplant One 890kW (1200hp) Wright R-1820-60 Cyclone nine-cylinder air-cooled radial engine
Speed: 406km/h (253mph)
Range: 1875km (1165 miles)
Ceiling: 9022m (29,600ft)
Crew: 2
Armament: Two 12.7mm (0.5in) M2 Browning machine guns fixed forward firing in cowling, one 7.62mm (0.30in) M1919 Browning machine gun flexibly mounted in rear cockpit; up to 544kg (1200lb) bombload

---

scoring several victories in the process.

The Marine corps were the first to fly the SBD, with VMB-2 receiving their first examples in late 1940. Ultimately, 20 Marine squadrons would fly the Dauntless and the SBD would persist in use with the Marines even after it had disappeared from USN units. By the end

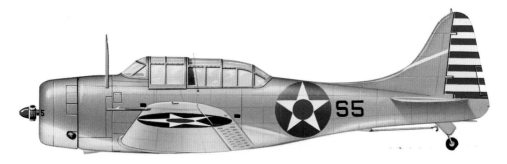

of 1941 the first US Navy SBDs were assigned to VB-6 aboard USS *Enterprise* and VB-2 on USS *Lexington.* At this stage the SBD's intended successor – the SB2C – was already flying and the Dauntless was regarded as something of a stopgap until the new aircraft could be brought into service. Production built up rapidly, and on 7 December 1941 roughly half of all aircraft aboard the US carrier fleet were SBDs. The 7 December also saw the combat debut of the Dauntless and it was not auspicious: 18 SBDs flew off *Enterprise* intending to transit to Ford Island Naval station

in Hawaii and happened to fly into the path of Japanese strike aircraft on their way to attack Pearl Harbor. Seven SBDs were lost to Japanese aircraft and 'friendly fire' from anti-aircraft guns. The tables turned quickly though – SBDs of *Enterprise's* air group found and sank the Japanese submarine I-70 on 10 December, the first enemy vessel to be sunk by US air attack.

Development of the SBD immediately preceding the US entry into the war was prompted by France, which had ordered an improved Dauntless with self-sealing tanks, crew armour and an armoured windscreen, features that the early fighting over Europe had proved to be essential to combat survival. None of the aircraft in the French order would be delivered by the time France fell, but the new variant entered US service

Douglas SBD-3 Dauntless

The yellow outline to the national markings on this SBD denotes its participation in Operation Torch, the Allied invasion of northern Africa in November 1942. This VS-41 Dauntless was operating from USS *Ranger.*

Douglas SBD-3 Dauntless

This SBD of VS-8 is seen in its early war scheme, retaining rudder stripes and red circles in the national insignia. By the time of the Battle of Midway in June 1942, all red markings had been removed.

Douglas SBD-3

Weight: (Maximum take-off) 4699kg (10360lb)
Dimensions: Length: 9.78m (32ft 1in), Wingspan: 12.66m (41ft 6in), Height: 4.14m (13ft 7in)
Powerplant One 890kW (1200hp) Wright R-1820-60 Cyclone nine-cylinder air-cooled radial engine
Speed: 404km/h (251 mph)
Range: 2220km (1380 miles)
Ceiling: 8310m (27260ft)
Crew: 2
Armament: Two 12.7mm (0.5in) M2 Browning machine guns fixed forward firing in cowling, two 7.62mm (0.30in) M1919 Browning machine guns flexibly mounted in rear cockpit; up to 544kg (1200lb) bombload

Cockpit
Dive bombing requires that the pilot aim the bombs
using the whole aircraft, unlike level bombing which
generally employs a specific member of the crew
to operate the bomb sight. The SBD was aimed
through a telescopic sight that passed through the
windscreen providing a 3x magnification.

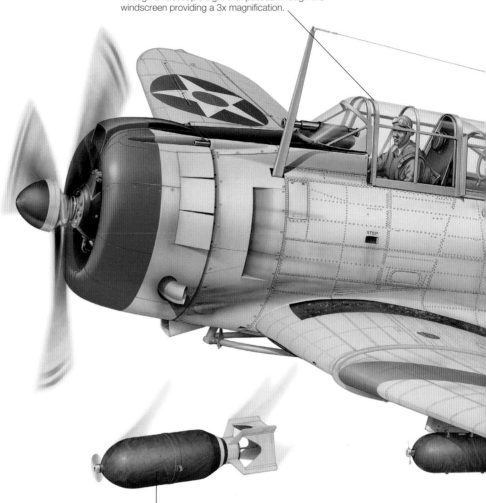

Payload
The SBD's bombload was relatively small, the
exact amount of ordnance carried depending
on how much fuel was required. This example
has just dropped its 227kg (500lb) bomb from
the centreline and has a 45kg (100lb) bomb
under each wing.

Rear armament
This early SBD is fitted with the standard early rear armament of a single hand held 7.62mm (0.3in) AN/M2 machine gun, a lightened version of the Browning M1919 intended for aircraft use. Later models would increase defensive armament to two such weapons.

Douglas SBD-1
This pre-war SBD-1 wears the markings of the commander of VMB-2, a US Marine Corps squadron based at San Diego, California, in early 1941. VMB-2 (later VMSB-232) was the first unit to receive the SBD in the latter part of 1940.

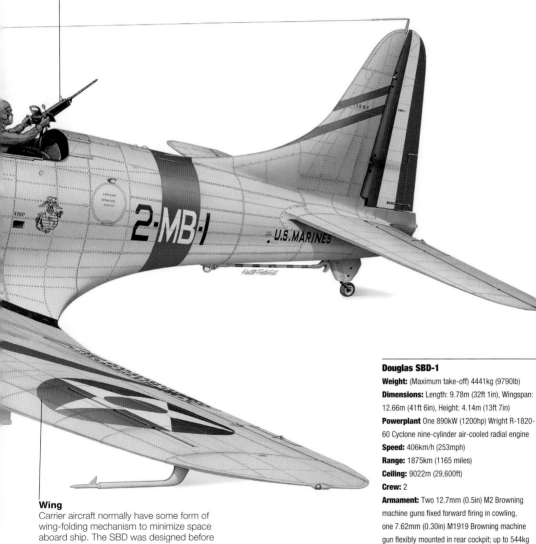

Wing
Carrier aircraft normally have some form of wing-folding mechanism to minimize space aboard ship. The SBD was designed before folding wings were the norm and never possessed such a feature.

Douglas SBD-1
Weight: (Maximum take-off) 4441kg (9790lb)
Dimensions: Length: 9.78m (32ft 1in), Wingspan: 12.66m (41ft 6in), Height: 4.14m (13ft 7in)
Powerplant One 890kW (1200hp) Wright R-1820-60 Cyclone nine-cylinder air-cooled radial engine
Speed: 406km/h (253mph)
Range: 1875km (1165 miles)
Ceiling: 9022m (29,600ft)
Crew: 2
Armament: Two 12.7mm (0.5in) M2 Browning machine guns fixed forward firing in cowling, one 7.62mm (0.30in) M1919 Browning machine gun flexibly mounted in rear cockpit; up to 544kg (1200lb) bombload

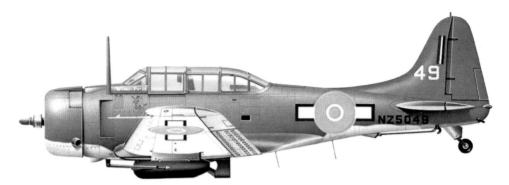

as the SBD-3, arguably the first truly combat-ready Dauntless. In total 584 SBD-3s would be built until October 1942, when production switched to the externally similar SBD-4 that differed primarily from earlier aircraft in featuring a 24 rather than a 12-volt electrical system. The SBD-4 also upgraded the

Douglas SBD-5

Weight: (Maximum take-off) 4853kg (10700lb)
Dimensions: Length: 10.09m (33ft 1in), Wingspan: 12.66m (41ft 6in), Height: 4.14m (13ft 7in)
Powerplant One 890kW (1200hp) Wright R-1820-60 Cyclone nine-cylinder air-cooled radial engine
Speed: 410km/h (255mph)
Range: 1794km (1115 miles)
Ceiling: 7780m (25,530ft)
Crew: 2
Armament: Two 12.7mm (0.5in) M2 Browning machine guns fixed forward firing in cowling, two 7.62mm (0.30in) M1919 Browning machine guns flexibly mounted in rear cockpit; up to two 1020kg (2250lb) bombload

defensive armament to a pair of 7.6mm (0.3in) machine guns in the rear cockpit and 780 were constructed.

Operation Torch

The last Dauntless variant to see operational service from carriers was the SBD-5, of which 2965 were built between February 1943 and April 1944. This variant featured a more powerful R-1820-60 Cyclone that mitigated the effect of the increasing weight of the aircraft as more equipment was added. By the time the SBD-5 began to appear on carrier decks the SBD had already fought its way through the most decisive battles of the Pacific war, destroying six Japanese carriers in the process, three within the space of six minutes at the Battle of Midway, arguably the most decisive naval battle of the Pacific war. SBDs also saw action in the west, playing an important role in the Operation Torch landings as well

Douglas SBD-5 Dauntless

The RNZAF received 41 SBDs, the aircraft being used solely by 25 Squadron before conversion to the F4U. NZ5049 named 'WINNI-PU-III' was based at Piva, on the Bougainville Islands, in April 1944 and was returned to the USMC in the following month.

Douglas SBD-5 Dauntless

The French made extensive use of the SBD. This SBD-5 was serving with *Aeronvale* unit *Flotille* 4FB at Cognac in January of 1945 for operations against pockets of German resistance in Southern France. The SBDs were worked hard: by April, French Dauntlesses were averaging three missions per day.

as sinking five ships in Bodø harbour, Norway, during Operation Leader. The last major battle in which SBDs played a major part was the Battle of the Philippine Sea in June 1944, and the Dauntless was supplanted on US carrier decks by the end of the year, although Marine Corps units kept flying the Dauntless until the end of the war. Interestingly, throughout its whole career this archetypal carrier aircraft was never fitted with folding wings.

A-24 Banshee

As well as its service in the US Navy and Marine Corps, the Dauntless also saw combat usage with the USAAF as the A-24 Banshee, of which 1200 were ordered, although only around half were delivered after it had proved horrifically vulnerable in service. This was in stark contrast to USN experience, where somewhat surprisingly the SBD had the lowest loss rate of any US naval aircraft in the Pacific. The different experiences of the SBD and A-24 can be at least partly explained by the different tactics employed by the Army. The USAAF favoured a glide-bombing attack rather than the near vertical dive of the USN, and the aircraft was more vulnerable to fighters and ground fire as a direct result. The Banshees also tended to be sent on missions without fighter escort, which proved costly. A disastrous July 1942 mission over New Guinea in which

five of seven attacking A-24s were shot down by A6M Zeros and another so badly damaged it was forced to crash land prompted the Air Force to remove the A-24 from combat in the Pacific, although more powerful A-24Bs, roughly equivalent to the SBD-5, continued on operations against Japanese forces in the Aleutians until 1943.

The Royal Navy considered ordering the Dauntless but rejected it after testing nine examples during 1943, although the RNZAF took on 41 second-hand SBDs, equipping one squadron with them that saw combat in the New Hebrides (now Vanuatu) during the first half of 1944 before New Zealand's Dauntlesses were replaced by the more potent F4U Corsair. Chile and Mexico both flew A-24s for coastal patrol work but saw no combat, in contrast to French Dauntlesses that saw much action. Denied receiving the SBD-3 due to the German victory of 1940, the Free French Air Force and Naval aviation units received around 80 SBD-5 and A-24Bs during 1943 and 44. French Air Force units initially utilized their Dauntlesses and Banshees for coastal patrol work before flying them in support of Operation Dragoon – the invasion of Southern France.

Following this, the aircraft were heavily committed to attacking German-occupied cities along the Atlantic coast. Although air force SBDs and A-24s had

Douglas SBD-5

Weight: (Maximum take-off) 4853kg (10700lb)
Dimensions: Length: 10.09m (33ft 1in), Wingspan: 12.66m (41ft 6in), Height: 4.14m (13ft 7in)
Powerplant One 890kW (1200hp) Wright R-1820-60 Cyclone nine-cylinder air-cooled radial engine
Speed: 410km/h (255mph)
Range: 1794km (1115 miles)
Ceiling: 7780m (25,530ft)
Crew: 2
Armament: Two 12.7mm (0.5in) M2 Browning machine guns fixed forward firing in cowling, two 7.62mm (0.30in) M1919 Browning machine guns flexibly mounted in rear cockpit; up to two 1020kg (2250lb) bombload

been relegated to training by 1946, the French Navy continued to operate the aircraft and these would be the last Dauntlesses to see combat, flying in support of French troops from the carrier *Arromanches* during the Indochina War, although by 1949 the SBD had been withdrawn from combat operations. The last Dauntless trainers were taken out of French service in 1953.

Cutaway key

1 Aerial stub
2 Rudder balance
3 Rudder upper hinge
4 Rudder frame
5 Rudder tab
6 Rudder lower hinge
7 Tailfin structure
8 Port elevator
9 Port tailplane
10 Tailfin root fillet
11 Frame
12 Fuselage frame/ tailfin pick-up
13 Tailplane spar attachment
14 Tailplane structure
15 Elevator torque tube
16 Tail navigation light
17 Elevator tab hinge fairing
18 Elevator hinge
19 Elevator tab
20 Elevator frame
21 Elevator outer hinge
22 Tailplane forward spar
23 Fixed tailwheel
pneumatic tyre
on A-24 versions)
24 Arresting hook uplock
25 Fuselage frame
26 Lift point
27 Arrestor hook (extended)
28 Tie-down ring
29 Arresting hook pivot
30 Control cables
31 Fuselage structure
32 Bulkhead
33 Section light
34 Radio bay
35 Radio bay access door
36 Wingroot fairing frame
37 Stringers
38 Life-raft cylindrical stowage (access door
portside)
39 Dorsal armament stowage
40 Hinged doors
41 Aerial
42 Twin 7.62mm (.30in) Browning
machine-guns
43 Gunner's face armour
44 Canopy aft-sliding section (open)
45 Gun mounting
46 Ammunition feed
47 Canopy aft-sliding section (closed)
48 Ammunition box
49 Oxygen cylinder
50 Oxygen rebreather
51 Oxygen spare cylinder
52 Entry hand/foothold
53 Aft cockpit floor
54 Radio controls
55 Gunner's position
56 Gun mounting
57 Canopy fixed centre-section
58 Wind deflector
59 Armoured centre bulkhead
60 Angled support frame
61 Gunner's emergency flight controls
62 Control direct linkage
63 Hydraulics controls
64 Entry hand/foothold
65 Oxygen rebreather
66 Map case
67 Pilot's seat and harness

68 Back armour
69 Catapult headrest
70 Canopy forward-sliding section
71 Compass
72 Perforated dive flap
73 Aerial mast
74 Aileron tab
75 Port aileron
76 Aileron tab control linkage
77 Port formation light
78 Port navigation light
79 Pitot head
80 Fixed wing slots
81 Wing skinning
82 Underwing ASB radar antenna (retrofit)
83 Port outer wing fuel tank (55 US-gal/
208 litre capacity)
84 Aileron control rod
85 Telescopic sight

86 Windscreen
87 Armoured inner panel
88 Instrument panel shroud
89 Two 12.7mm (.50in) machineguns
90 Control column
91 Switch panel
92 Instrument panel
93 Case ejection chute
94 Ammunition box

95 Engine bearer upper attachment
96 Armoured deflection plate
97 Machine-gun barrel shrouds
98 Engine bearers
99 Oil tank
100 Exhaust slot
101 Oil cooler
102 Cooling gills
103 Exhaust manifold

Douglas SBD-3 Dauntless

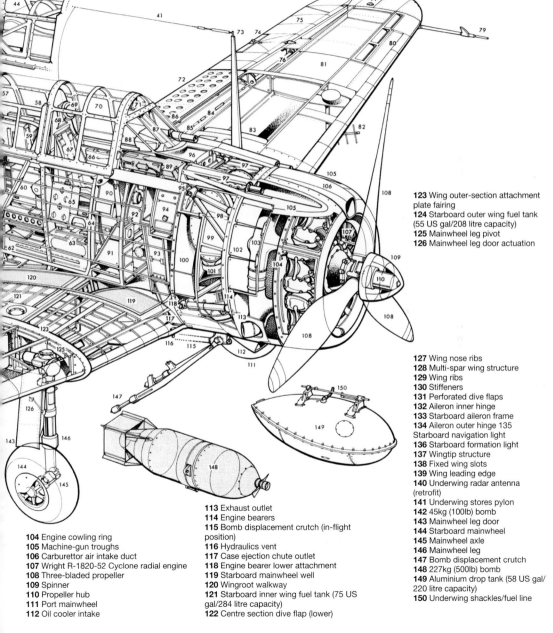

123 Wing outer-section attachment plate fairing
124 Starboard outer wing fuel tank (55 US gal/208 litre capacity)
125 Mainwheel leg pivot
126 Mainwheel leg door actuation

127 Wing nose ribs
128 Multi-spar wing structure
129 Wing ribs
130 Stiffeners
131 Perforated dive flaps
132 Aileron inner hinge
133 Starboard aileron frame
134 Aileron outer hinge 135 Starboard navigation light
136 Starboard formation light
137 Wingtip structure
138 Fixed wing slots
139 Wing leading edge
140 Underwing radar antenna (retrofit)
141 Underwing stores pylon
142 45kg (100lb) bomb
143 Mainwheel leg door
144 Starboard mainwheel
145 Mainwheel axle
146 Mainwheel leg
147 Bomb displacement crutch
148 227kg (500lb) bomb
149 Aluminium drop tank (58 US gal/ 220 litre capacity)
150 Underwing shackles/fuel line

113 Exhaust outlet
114 Engine bearers
115 Bomb displacement crutch (in-flight position)
116 Hydraulics vent
117 Case ejection chute outlet
118 Engine bearer lower attachment
119 Starboard mainwheel well
120 Wingroot walkway
121 Starboard inner wing fuel tank (75 US gal/284 litre capacity)
122 Centre section dive flap (lower)

104 Engine cowling ring
105 Machine-gun troughs
106 Carburettor air intake duct
107 Wright R-1820-52 Cyclone radial engine
108 Three-bladed propeller
109 Spinner
110 Propeller hub
111 Port mainwheel
112 Oil cooler intake

North American B-25B

North American's B-25 medium bomber was an exceptional aircraft, but never intended for carrier operations. Despite this it performed one of the most famous carrier-launched missions in aviation history.

Following the attack on Pearl Harbor, the Americans decided to strike back at the Japanese mainland. It was Captain Francis S. Low who devised the idea of using USAAF bombers launched from a Navy carrier to do it. The B-25B was selected as it combined a wingspan short enough (just) to clear the carrier's island with a brief enough takeoff run to make a carrier launch feasible. The USS *Hornet,* then undertaking trials in the Atlantic, was the newest and fastest carrier in the fleet and was selected to carry the attack force and the B-25 crews under the leadership of prewar racing pilot Colonel James Doolittle. Pilots practised making takeoffs from an outline of the carrier painted on a runway at Eglin Field. On 2 February 1942 the first test launch of a B-25 from USS *Hornet* took place as the crews continued to practice short takeoffs ashore. The B-25s were modified with collapsible 265-gallon fuel tanks in

the bomb bay, the heavy (and secret) Norden bombsights were discarded and new propellers fitted. Famously, the ventral defensive guns were discarded, to be replaced by painted broomsticks as decoy weapons in the tailcone. On 2 April the *Hornet* departed San Franscisco with 16 B-25Bs lashed to her deck. Even at this stage the modifications were incomplete and the Navy blimp L-8 was used to ferry further B-25 parts to *Hornet* at sea.

Propaganda success

The carrier was spotted by Japanese vessels on 18 April and forced to launch the strike early. All 16 B-25s took off successfully and attacked a variety of targets in Japan, including Tokyo and the Yokosuka dockyards, before flying on to crash-land in China. The damage caused was materially insignificant but the psychological effect was immense, particularly on

An Army Air Force B-25B bomber takes off from USS *Hornet* at the start of the raid, 18 April 1942.

North American B-25B

Weight: (Maximum takeoff) 12,909kg (28,460lb)
Dimensions: Length: 16.13m (52ft 11in),
Wingspan: 20.6m (67ft 7in), Height: 4.8m (15ft 9in)
Powerplant: Two kW (1700hp) Wright R-2600-9
Cyclone 14-cylinder, air-cooled, radial piston engine
Speed: 518km/h (322mph)
Range: 3220km (2000 miles)
Ceiling: 7163m (23,500ft)
Crew: 5
Armament: Two 12.7mm (0.5in) Browning in dorsal
turret, two 12.7mm (0.5in) Browning in ventral
turret (deleted for Doolittle raid), one 7.62mm (0.3in)
Browning M1919 machine gun flexibly mounted in
nose; up to 1361kg (3000lb) bombload

---

the morale of the US population. This would not be the only time non-naval aircraft would operate off an aircraft carrier during World War II, but was by far the most dramatic.

Fairey Barracuda

Through no fault of its own, the Barracuda was seriously delayed and underpowered. Despite this, it proved tough and effective in various roles and played a major part in Fleet Air Arm operations for the last two years of the war.

The origins of the Barracuda lie in Specification S.24/37, issued by the Air Ministry in October 1937, for a monoplane replacement for the company's own as yet unbuilt Fairey Albacore. Two prototypes were ordered in September 1938 to be powered by the promising new 24-cylinder Rolls-Royce Exe, which by November 1938 had entered flight testing in a modified Fairey Battle. The first of several delays to the Barracuda programme came as a result of Rolls-Royce's decision to abandon Exe development, among other engines, to concentrate on the Merlin and Griffon.

After various alternative powerplants such as the Napier Sabre and Fairey's own experimental P.24 were rejected, Marcel Lobelle's design team, under heavy pressure from the Air Ministry, were forced to utilize the Rolls-Royce Merlin 30 that offered only just over half the power of the Sabre or P.24 and was barely adequate for the Barracuda's needs.

Typically for a naval aircraft of this era, the Barracuda was intended to perform several functions. As

well as torpedo and dive bombing it would be expected to undertake reconnaissance and spotting duties with the various equipment required for each role having to be crammed into the airframe somewhere. As a result, the unladen weight of the Barracuda grew inexorably. Nonetheless the Air Ministry were suitably impressed with the design and ordered 300 'off the drawing board' in August 1939.

Production delays

Work on the prototypes proceeded slowly due to the progress of the war. During the summer of 1940, defensive fighter types received the utmost priority and the Barracuda was delayed again. The first prototype eventually making its maiden flight on 7 December 1940. During testing it was found that turbulent airflow in the wake of the large flaps when they were deployed caused severe buffeting of the tailplane, and deck landing, first achieved on 18 May, was considered dangerous. The issue was solved by moving the tailplane to a high-set position near the top of the vertical

Fairey Barracuda Mk.II

LS542 was aboard HMS *Victorious* in early 1944, serving with 829 Squadron. In April 1944, this aircraft was one of 42 Barracudas to dive bomb and heavily damage the German battleship *Tirpitz* at anchor in Kaafjord, Norway, during Operation Tungsten.

Fairey Barracuda Mk II

Weight: (Maximum takeoff) 6396kg (14100lb)
Dimensions: Length: 12.12m (39ft 9in), Wingspan: 14.99m (49ft 2in), Height: 4.62m (15ft 2in)
Powerplant: One 1220kW (1640hp) Rolls-Royce Merlin 32 V-12 liquid-cooled piston engine
Speed: 390km/h (240mph)
Range: 1850km (1150 miles)
Ceiling: 4900m (16,000ft)
Crew: 3
Armament: Two 7.7mm (0.303in) Vickers K machine guns flexibly mounted in rear cockpit; one 735kg (1620lb) torpedo or four 205kg (450lb) depth charges or up to 660kg (1500lb) bombload

fin, resulting in one of the Barracuda's most distinctive features. Testing was further delayed when the prototype's undercarriage was retracted while taxiing, damaging the engine. It wasn't until February 1942 that handling and performance trials were completed.

Two months later the first Barracuda Mk.Is began to roll off the production line. Fairey had been in talks with Rolls-Royce about the possibility of fitting an engine of greater power than the Merlin 30, potentially considering the Griffon IIB that was being developed

The Barracuda used its Youngman flaps as dive brakes. These can be seen in this dramatic press photograph behind the trailing edge of the wing, angled slightly up to control speed in the dive. When angled down the flaps increased lift at low speed making the Barracuda a docile deck landing aircraft.

P1767 was the prototype Barracuda and is seen here after the horizontal tail surfaces were moved to the top of the fin. Early problems with the exhaust system and hydraulics led to a series of apparently inexplicable fatal crashes.

beyond: final Barracuda combat sorties took place on 1 September to attack Japanese shipping near Hong Kong, defying the ceasefire.

for the Firefly. This engine was in short supply so Rolls-Royce suggested the Merlin 32 instead, which offered around a third more power than the Merlin 30. It was decided that the Barracuda Mk.II featuring the improved engine and a four-bladed propeller would enter production as soon as possible, thus only 25 Mk.Is were built. A shortage of propellers delayed production yet again but the Mk.II would be produced in large numbers to become the first variant to see action. The Mk.II was also equipped with ASV IIN radar as standard with distinctive Yagi aerials towards the tip of each wing.

First combat operations

The first operational Barracuda unit, 827 Squadron, began to receive their aircraft, a mixture of Mks.I and II, in January 1943 to replace the Albacore. A further 10 units formed throughout the year and the Barracuda quickly supplanted the Albacore and Swordfish on fleet carrier decks. The first combat operations were flown during early 1944, mixed flights of torpedo- and bomb-armed Barracudas conducting a series of anti-shipping strikes along the Norwegian coast with impressive results – by the end of May Barracudas had accounted for 14 ships sunk and 18 damaged. Operation Tungsten was a significant early mission when four Barracuda squadrons attacked

the German battleship *Tirpitz* inflicting heavy damage, although the battleship remained afloat.

Far East deployment

The majority of the Barracuda's operational career took place in the Far East, beginning with the successful strikes on Japanese-held refineries in Sabang, Sumatra, and followed by numerous attacks on Japanese positions in both the Pacific and Indian oceans. Unfortunately, the high temperatures that prevailed in the Pacific theatre degraded the Barracuda's performance, with combat range being reduced reputedly by as much as 30 per cent. The Merlin 32 as fitted to the Barracuda was optimized for low-altitude, and this also caused problems. Strikes against targets in Eastern Java required flying over Indonesian mountain ranges for example, and the Barracuda did not possess sufficient altitude performance to achieve this. As a result, the decision was taken to re-equip torpedo squadrons of the British Pacific Fleet with the Grumman TBF Avenger, although this process would not be completed by the end of the conflict. On VJ Day the carriers of the British Pacific Fleet still possessed four Barracuda squadrons alongside five of Avengers, and the Barracuda fought until the end of the war, and indeed

Anti-submarine warfare

Efforts to optimize the Barracuda for anti-submarine warfare resulted in the Mk.III, of which 852 were constructed, which differed primarily from the Mk.II in mounting the ASV III radar in a semi-retractable blister under the rear fuselage. A more thorough redesign was undertaken to deal with the Barracuda's acknowledged lack of power when a Mk.II was fitted with a Rolls-Royce Griffon to become the prototype Mk.IV that first flew in November 1944. A decision to replace the Barracuda with the Fairey Spearfish saw the Mk.IV abandoned, but serious delays in the Spearfish programme (which, in the event, would never progress to production) saw the development of the stop-gap Barracuda Mk.V featuring a Griffon 37, redesigned wing and centre section, fin and rudder of increased area, strengthened undercarriage and an aerodynamically cleaned-up airframe. The Griffon finally blessed the Barracuda with the power it required and performance was much improved, but the Mk.V was just too late to see service in World War II and only 37 were built. After the war Barracudas remained in service until 1953, the last being anti-submarine Mk.IIIs. In addition to its service with the Royal Navy, the Barracuda also operated post-war with the Royal Canadian Navy and French Air Force.

Curtiss SB2C Helldiver

The Curtiss SB2C Helldiver weathered a protracted development, problematic service introduction, and an appalling reputation to become one of the most successful naval aircraft of the war.

Intended as a replacement for the SBD Dauntless with higher top speed, greater range and an internal bomb bay, the XSB2C first flew on 18 December 1940. Confident in the design experience of Curtiss, the US Navy had already ordered 370 production aircraft in November despite wind tunnel data suggesting that the aircraft would possess poor handling characteristics and an unacceptably high stalling speed. Flight testing of the XSB2C revealed that the wind tunnel predictions were correct and thus began nearly three years of alterations before the aircraft was put, prematurely, into service. The problems were manifold but mostly derived from the fact that the SB2C's dimensions were dictated by the need for it to fit on an Essex class carrier's deck lift. The aircraft was essentially too small for its weight and the prototype exhibited structural weaknesses, poor handling, directional instability and unpleasant stall characteristics. There were also initially problems with the Wright R-2600 engine but this, at least, matured into a reliable powerplant relatively quickly.

Engine failure

After the XSB2C crashed on 8 February 1941 due to engine failure on approach to land, Curtiss took the opportunity to rebuild it with a slightly lengthened fuselage and a much larger tail, the huge fin and rudder becoming a distinctive feature of the type. The prototype was lost on 21 December 1941, permanently this time, due to the wing failing in diving tests, although the pilot managed to achieve a successful landing. The issues with the prototype had prompted the Navy to demand the unprecedented number of 880 design changes to the first production model, delaying the appearance of the aircraft (although all the changes would only be incorporated in the 601st aircraft off the production line). While some of the changes improved the problems of the SB2C, others – such as increasing the installed armament and adding a greater fuel capacity – added weight to the already overweight aircraft and further exacerbated handling issues. The delays increased and resulted in the Grumman TBF entering service before the SB2C, despite the fact the Grumman aircraft had begun its

Curtiss SB2C-5

Postwar usage of the SB2C by the US was relatively brief, the Helldiver serving in reserve units until 1950. This SB2C-5 was based at Glenview Naval Air Station, Illinois, in 1948.

Curtiss SB2C-5

Weight: (Maximum takeoff) 7388kg (16287lb)
Dimensions: Length: 11.18m (36ft 8in), Wingspan: 15.16m (49ft 9in), Height: 4.01m (13ft 2in)
Powerplant: One 1400kW (1900hp) Wright R-2600-20 Twin Cyclone 14-cylinder air-cooled radial piston engine
Speed: 475km/h (295mph)
Range: 1875km (1165 miles)
Ceiling: 8900m (29,100ft)
Crew: 2
Armament: Two 20mm (0.79in) AN/M2 cannon fixed forward-firing in wings, two 7.62mm (0.3in) M1919 Browning machine guns flexibly mounted in rear cockpit; up to 910kg (2000lb) bombload or one 910kg (2000lb) Mark XIII torpedo in internal bomb bay, 452kg (1000lb) bombload on wing racks or eight 127mm (5in) high-velocity aircraft rockets

---

development a full two years later. So serious were the problems and delays attendant on the SB2C programme that Curtiss-Wright were investigated by the Senate War Investigating committee

Curtiss SB2C-4

Weight: (Maximum takeoff) 7710kg (16997lb)
Dimensions: Length: 11.18m (36ft 8in), Wingspan: 15.16m (49ft 9in), Height: 4.01m (13ft 2in)
Powerplant: One 1400kW (1900hp) Wright R-2600-20 Twin Cyclone 14-cylinder air-cooled radial piston engine
Speed: 475km/h (295mph)
Range: 1875km (1165 miles)
Ceiling: 8900m (29,100ft)
Crew: 2
Armament: Two 20mm (0.79in) AN/M2 cannon fixed forward-firing in wings, two 7.62mm (0.3in) M1919 Browning machine guns flexibly mounted in rear cockpit; up to 910kg (2000lb) bombload or one 910kg (2000lb) Mark XIII torpedo in internal bomb bay, 452kg (1000lb) bombload on wing racks or eight 127mm (5in) high-velocity aircraft rockets

headed by the future President Truman. The report it delivered was scathing and is believed to have hastened the ultimate demise of the company.

The Beast

The initial SB2C-1 production version was built only in relatively small numbers as it was deemed unsuitable for combat and virtually all were retained in the US for training, although one Marine Corps unit did end up flying SB2C-1s (converted from USAAF A-25s) operationally from Enewetak Atoll. The SB2C-1C was the first version to see combat when Helldivers of VB-17 flying from USS *Bunker Hill* attacked the port of Rabaul on 11 November 1943. The aircraft was proving unpopular with crews who invariably compared it against the SBD Dauntless it replaced

Curtiss SB2C-4

This Helldiver was operated by VB-3, the 'Black Panthers' aboard USS *Yorktown*, as signified by the white panel on the vertical tail, in early 1945. *Yorktown* was covering the landings on Iwo Jima at this time, as part of Task Force 58.

Curtiss SB2C-1C

Serving aboard USS *Bunker Hill* covering operations over Saipan in June 1944, this SB2C-1C was on the strength of VB-8. This unit had replaced VB-17, the very first USN SB2C squadron, aboard the carrier. These early Helldivers proved extremely unpopular with crews.

and found the SB2C wanting for it was considerably more difficult to fly and particularly deck land. It was overweight and underpowered, and although it could carry a greater bombload than the SBD and was faster, it possessed a shorter range and was a less accurate dive bomber than the Dauntless. Furthermore, at this stage the Helldiver was still a distinctly immature combat aircraft, suffered from an unreliable electrical and hydraulic system and was subject to failures brought about by suspect build quality: on at least one occasion an arrested landing tore the entire aircraft in two. Crews joked that SB2C stood for 'Son of a Bitch 2nd Class' and nicknamed the aircraft 'the Beast'.

Appalling handling

Curtiss also received an order for 900 land-based versions called the A-25 Shrike for the USAAF, but by the time they were entering service in late 1943 the Air Force were discarding dive-bombers for fighter-bombers and transferred 410 to the Marine Corps

as SB2C-1s. Around the same time the Royal Navy and RAAF ordered 450 and 150 examples respectively, but both services cancelled their orders after testing the aircraft, the Royal Navy report citing 'appalling handling'. As a result only the US would fly the Helldiver operationally during World War II.

Things started to improve with the SB2C-3, which featured a more powerful R-2600-20 engine and four-bladed propeller. The extra power available from this engine largely mitigated the handling issues and increased the top speed by 21km/h (13mph) to 473km/h (294mph). Dive bombing accuracy problems had been traced to the dive brakes, which caused tailplane buffet when opened. The fitting of perforated dive brakes solved that problem quite easily once the cause had been traced. APS-4 radar was fitted to a few examples of this variant in a pod under the starboard wing, these aircraft being designated SB2C-3E; the same fitting was applied to examples of later variants. Build

A Curtiss SB2C-5 Helldiver of VB-10, USS *Intrepid* (CV-11), flies over Tientsin, China, as the city is reoccupied by the Allies, 5 September 1945.

quality issues had by now been cured, although their reputation lingered, and the Helldiver at last began to show its potential in combat and started to replace the SBD in earnest: in February 1944 only USS *Bunker Hill* carried Helldivers, but by June five squadrons on five carriers were equipped with the SB2C and in the same month it played a significant part in the Battle of the Philippine Sea, proving highly formidable.

The most numerous Helldiver model was the SB2C-4 that incorporated every improvement of the SB2C-3 and added eight zero-length rocket launchers under the wings as targets were increasingly shore-based. The final variant to see production was the SB2C-5 that differed principally in possessing increased fuel capacity. An up-engined SB2C-6 was flown but cancelled due to the end of the war and

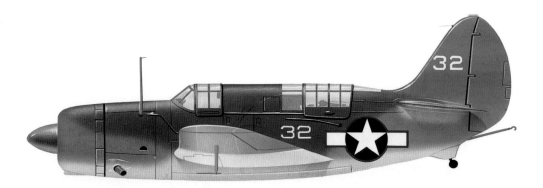

Curtiss SB2C-1C

Weight: (Maximum takeoff) 7388kg (16287lb)

Dimensions: Length: 11.18m (36ft 8in), Wingspan: 15.16m (49ft 9in), Height: 4.01m (13ft 2in)

Powerplant: One 1400kW (1900hp) Wright R-2600-20 Twin Cyclone 14-cylinder air-cooled radial piston engine

Speed: 462km/h (287mph)

Range: 1786km (1110 miles)

Ceiling: 7370m (24179ft)

Crew: 2

Armament: Two 20mm (0.79in) AN/M2 cannon fixed forward-firing in wings, two 7.62mm (0.3in) M1919 Browning machine guns flexibly mounted in rear cockpit; up to 910kg (2000lb) bombload or one 910kg (2000lb) Mark XIII torpedo in internal bomb bay

a tricycle gear development, the SB3C, was designed by Curtiss but never built. In total 7140 had been built, with several hundred produced in Canada by Fairchild and the Canadian Car & Foundry company.

Reserve unit service

After the war the Helldiver persisted in US units for a time but all were withdrawn from US carriers during 1947, although the aircraft would serve in reserve units for a few years after that. This was not the end of the combat career of the Helldiver though, as Greek examples would see action during the Greek Civil War against Communist ground forces in 1949. Later still, French SB2C-5s aboard the carriers *Arromanches, Bois Belleau* and *La Fayette* flew missions against Viet Minh forces during the First Indochina War, culminating in the decisive Battle of Dien Bien Phu. The final operator of all was Italy who retired their last Helldivers in 1959.

Curtiss SB2C-1C

VB-17 was the debut Helldiver squadron, seeing action for the first time on 11 November 1943 when they attacked the Japanese port of Rabaul in New Britain. This Helldiver is depicted as it appeared slightly earlier, as demonstrated by the red outlined markings which were dropped in August 1943.

Curtiss SB2C

Operating as part of Task Force 58, the Helldivers assigned to USS *Hancock* flew strikes against Japanese ground targets in support of the landings on Iwo Jima during February 1945. By this time the Helldiver had matured into a reliable and effective combat aircraft.

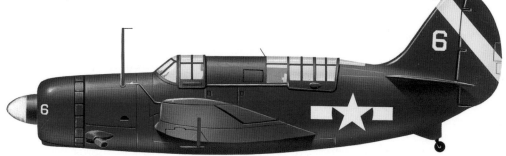

Brewster SB2A Buccaneer

Considered one of the most disappointing aircraft of World War II, Brewster's Buccaneer was produced in large numbers but never saw operational service.

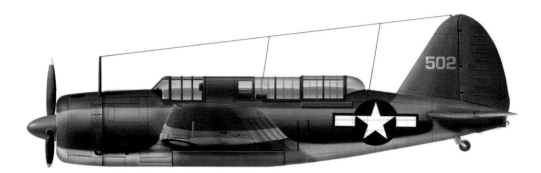

Built to the same US Navy specification that resulted in the Curtiss SB2C Helldiver, itself an aircraft hardly free of problems, Brewster's Model B-340 turned out to be overweight, underpowered and lacking in manoeuvrability but initially attracted considerable interest from export customers.

The first customer was France, which ordered 192 examples designated the B-340-F, with an option for a further 258 in May 1940. After the fall of France, the UK took over the order and increased the total to 750 in October, giving the aircraft the name Bermuda. Unfortunately, production was seriously delayed and the British found the aircraft wanting when RAF test pilots finally got to fly an example in February 1942. Meanwhile, the Netherlands East Indies ordered 192 examples for the close support role. Sadly for Brewster, Dutch resistance to the Japanese collapsed before any could be delivered and aircraft completed to this contract were split between the UK and USA.

Testing by the RAF found that the Bermuda was 'unfit for operational

use' but the RAF agreed to continue accepting Bermudas to allow the Brewster assembly line to keep functioning until Corsair licence production could begin. Ultimately, they received 206 Bermudas, none of which ever served with any unit. In the US the Brewster, designated SB2A and named Buccaneer by the Navy, was rated 'satisfactory' during carrier trials but general performance left much to be desired and the aircraft never served with an operational unit.

Trainer

However, the SB2A was employed briefly but quite extensively as a lead-in trainer for Naval and Marine Corps crews transitioning to the SB2C and night fighter versions of the F4U Corsair and F6F Hellcat at a time when these aircraft were in short supply. Stripped of military equipment for the training role, the Buccaneer possessed decent performance and was an effective bridge between the SNJ trainer and operational types. The USAAF also received a few Brewsters, designating them the A-34, and utilized them briefly for target towing.

Brewster SB2A-3 Buccaneer

White 502 was one of many USN Buccaneers utilized in the advanced training role, a task at which it performed well enough, being of similar performance and size to the types that aircrews would take into action. However, the production of 771 of these disappointing aircraft was questionable at best.

Brewster SB2A-4 Buccaneer

Weight: (Maximum takeoff) 6481kg (14289lb)

Dimensions: Length: 11.94m (39ft 2in), Wingspan: 14.33m (47ft), Height: 4.7m (15ft 5in)

Powerplant: One 1268kW (1700hp) Wright R-2600 Twin Cyclone 14-cylinder air-cooled radial piston engine

Speed: 441km/h (273mph)

Range: 2696km (1675 miles)

Ceiling: 7590m (24,900ft)

Crew: 2

Armament: Two 12.7mm (0.5in) M2 Browning machine guns fixed forward-firing in fuselage, two 7.62mm (0.3in) M1919 Browning machine guns fixed forward firing in wings, two 7.62mm (0.3in) M1919 Browning machine guns flexibly mounted in rear cockpit, up to 226kg (500lb) bombload in internal bomb bay and 226kg (500lb) bombload on wing racks

---

Grumman TBF Avenger

Grumman's first attempt at designing a torpedo bomber, the versatile TBF Avenger was generally considered to be the best aircraft in its class during the war and was produced in large numbers.

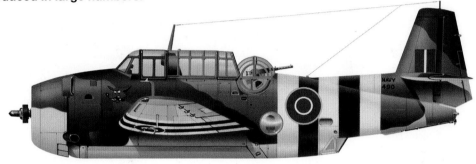

By 1939 it was becoming increasingly clear that the Douglas TBD was already falling behind world standards and a replacement would be required as a matter of urgency. The US Navy accordingly distributed a request for design proposals for a new torpedo bomber, stipulating the ability to carry a torpedo or other ordnance in an internal bomb bay, a range of 1609km (1000 miles) and a top speed of 483km (300mph). Two of the 13 designs submitted were selected as promising enough for further development: the Vought TBU and Grumman TBF – both would see production, although only one was destined to actually serve in combat.

Prototype

Ordered in March 1940, the first of two prototype Grumman XBTF-1s developed by a design team under Chief Engineer William Schwendler flew for the first time on 7 August 1941. Broadly resembling a scaled-up F4F Wildcat, the XTBF featured Grumman's patented STO-wing system that effectively reduced the size of this large aircraft for efficient storage aboard ship. The TBF was the heaviest

single-engine aircraft to see service during World War II, narrowly beating the P-47 Thunderbolt, and the largest to operate from a carrier deck during the conflict. The XBTF-1 featured a powered turret for defence, a first on a US Navy aircraft and unusual in that it was designed in-house by Grumman and electrically operated rather than the more usual mechanical or hydraulic turrets used in other aircraft.

The TBF was operated by a crew of three: the pilot, a turret gunner and a busy third crew member who occupied an unenviable position in the rear fuselage behind and below the turret and served as the bombardier, radioman and ventral gunner. Test flying proceeded swiftly with no major changes required to the airframe apart from a dorsal fin to impart better stability, the aircraft performing exactly as expected although top speed was only a disappointing 441km/h (274mph).

The first prototype was subsequently lost on 29 November 1941 when the Grumman test crew mistook a fine oil mist from a broken hydraulic line for smoke indicating an onboard fire and abandoned the

Grumman Avenger Mk.II

Although strongly associated with the war in the Pacific, the Avenger also served in Europe. This example in full invasion stripes was based at RNAS Donibristle during June 1944. In July, the Avenger scored its most unlikely victory when an RN example shot down a V-1 flying bomb.

Grumman Avenger Mk.II

Weight: (Maximum takeoff) 8115kg (17895lb)

Dimensions: Length: 12.2m (40ft), Wingspan: 16.51m (54ft 2in), Height: 5m (16ft 5in)

Powerplant: One 1300kW (1700hp) Wright R-2600-8 Twin Cyclone 14-cylinder air-cooled radial piston engine

Speed: 447km/h (278mph)

Range: 1456km (905 miles)

Ceiling: 6900m (22600ft)

Crew: 3

Armament: One 7.62mm (0.3in) M1919 Browning machine gun fixed forward-firing in nose; one 12.7mm (0.5in) M2 Browning machine gun in rear turret, one 7.62mm (0.3in) M1919 Browning machine gun flexibly mounted in ventral position; up to 907kg (2000lb) bombload or one 730kg (1670lb) torpedo in bomb bay

---

aircraft a mere 16km (10 miles) from Grumman's Bethpage plant. Luckily the construction of the second prototype was well under way. Slightly

Grumman TBF-1 Avenger

Weight: (Maximum takeoff) 8115kg (17895lb)
Dimensions: Length: 12.2m (40ft), Wingspan:
16.51m (54ft 2in), Height: 5m (16ft 5in)
Powerplant: One 1300kW (1700hp) Wright
R-2600-8 Twin Cyclone 14-cylinder air-cooled radial
piston engine
Speed: 447km/h (278mph)
Range: 1456km (905 miles)
Ceiling: 6900m (22600ft)
Crew: 3
Armament: One 7.62mm (0.3in) M1919 Browning
machine gun fixed forward-firing in nose; one
12.7mm (0.5in) M2 Browning machine gun in
rear turret, one 7.62mm (0.3in) M1919 Browning
machine gun flexibly mounted in ventral position; up
to 907kg (2000lb) bombload or one 907kg (2000lb)
Mark XIII torpedo or Mark 24 acoustic homing
torpedo in bomb bay

Grumman TBM-3 Avenger

By the time this General Motors built TBM-3 was
operating off USS *Randolph*, most of the Avenger's
missions were close support and level bombing
sorties rather than the torpedo attacks it was
designed for. In April 1945 *Randolph* was
part of Task Force 58 engaged in the invasion
of Okinawa.

earlier during October, in accordance
with a new USN policy of assigning
official names to aircraft the TBF
became the Avenger. A persistent but
understandable myth arose that the
Avenger was so named as a direct
response to the Pearl Harbor attack
when in fact it was merely a bizarrely
appropriate coincidence.

Weapon upgrade
Production went ahead with astonishing
speed, such that the first TBF-1s rolled
off the assembly line on 3 January 1942
and by June Grumman were building 60
TBFs a month, production exceeding
100 a month by November and would
continue to increase, reaching 150 per
month throughout 1943. After building
764 TBF-1s, Grumman switched to
the TBF-1C in which the single 7.6mm
(0.3in) nose gun was replaced with a
pair of 12.7mm (0.5in) Brownings. The

Grumman TBF-1 Avenger

This aircraft was the sole survivor of the Avenger's
disastrous combat debut when six VT-8 TBF-1s
from USS *Hornet,* on detachment to Midway Island,
attacked the Japanese fleet without fighter escort
on 4 June 1942.

Eastern Aircraft TBM-3

Weight: (Maximum takeoff) 8115kg (17895lb)
Dimensions: Length: 12.16m (39ft 11in), Wingspan:
16.51m (54ft 2in), Height: 5.02m (16ft 6in)
Powerplant: One 1417kW (1900hp) Wright
R-2600-20 Twin Cyclone 14-cylinder air-cooled
radial piston engine
Speed: 444km/h (276mph)
Range: 1626km (1010 miles)
Ceiling: 7090m (23261ft)
Crew: 3
Armament: Two 12.7mm (0.5in) M2 Browning
machine gun fixed forward-firing in wings; one
12.7mm (0.5in) M2 Browning machine gun in
rear turret, one 7.62mm (0.3in) M1919 Browning
machine gun flexibly mounted in ventral position; up
to 907kg (2000lb) bombload or one 907kg (2000lb)
Mark XIII torpedo or Mark 24 acoustic homing
torpedo in bomb bay

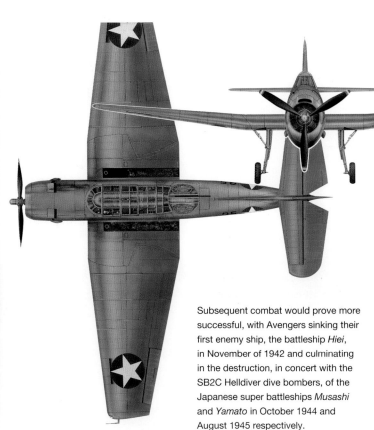

Grumman TBF-1 Avenger

Nicknamed 'Turkey' by its crews, the Avenger was an ungainly looking aircraft but what it lacked in aesthetic appeal it more than made up for in strength and combat effectiveness. This TBF-1 was one of the first built by Grumman's Bethpage factory.

the Royal Navy would receive over 921 Avengers and use them to equip 15 frontline squadrons, and although they would see some service on the Baltic convoys and in the Atlantic, the bulk of Royal Naval Avenger use took place in the Pacific. In total 63 Avengers also went to New Zealand to be used as bombers by the RNZAF, and these aircraft saw service during 1944 in support of the Bougainville campaign.

With the Avenger established in production and service it was clear that Grumman alone could not produce enough TBFs to meet demand. General Motors, who had suspended all automobile production on the outbreak of war, repurposed five car factories as the 'Eastern Aircraft Division' to supply aircraft components for the war effort, but before long were producing complete aircraft, the first being the F4F Wildcat and TBF Avenger. To assist with setting up production, Grumman supplied a complete TBF-1 to General Motors held together entirely with screws rather than rivets so it could be disassembled and reassembled at will. Eastern Aircraft would be responsible for around three quarters of Avenger production from November 1942. In US service they were referred to as the TBM and in Britain they became the Avenger Mk.II. The next major variant was the TBM-3, with a more powerful version of the R-2600 engine and featuring wing hardpoints for

Subsequent combat would prove more successful, with Avengers sinking their first enemy ship, the battleship *Hiei*, in November of 1942 and culminating in the destruction, in concert with the SB2C Helldiver dive bombers, of the Japanese super battleships *Musashi* and *Yamato* in October 1944 and August 1945 respectively.

Bougainville campaign

Meanwhile, the British Royal Navy were in desperate need of a modern torpedo bomber due to delays in the Fairey Barracuda programme, and began to receive deliveries of the TBF through lend-lease channels in August 1942. Originally named the Tarpon Mk.I in British service, the name was changed in January 1944 to Avenger TR Mk.I to match American practice and avoid confusion. The first frontline examples to see action were those of 832 squadron Fleet Air Arm which, surprisingly, was operating off USS *Saratoga* in support of US Marine landings in the Solomons. Ultimately

first service examples were delivered to VT-8 aboard USS *Hornet* by April 1942, becoming the first US aircraft to enter service after the US entered the war. *Hornet* was ordered into the Pacific before VT-8 could completely re-equip with TBFs and so sailed without the TBFs that they had so far received, six of these then being flown to Midway Island. The six Avengers subsequently became the first to go into combat and the first US Navy aircraft to engage the enemy at the Battle of Midway. Flying without fighter escort, the TBF's combat debut was decidedly inauspicious as five of the six were shot down and the sixth crash-landed, badly damaged, back on Midway.

Eastern Aircraft TBM-1C Avenger

7546 of the 9836 Avengers built in total would roll off the production lines of General Motors' Eastern Aircraft Division. This TBM-1C was serving with VT-4 on USS *Essex* during operations against Japanese targets on Formosa (now Taiwan) in January 1945.

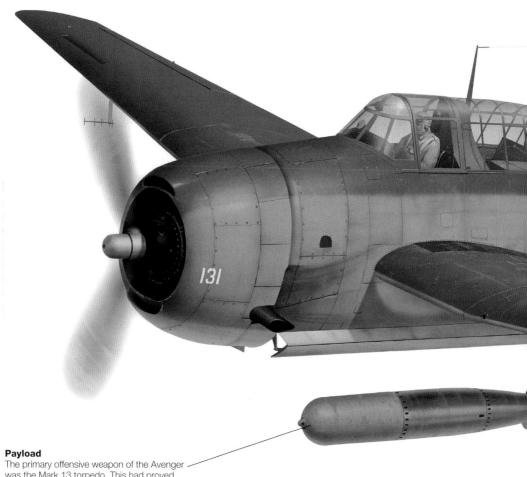

Payload
The primary offensive weapon of the Avenger was the Mark 13 torpedo. This had proved extremely unreliable during the first year of war but various improvements to aerodynamically stabilize the torpedo and cushion its entry into the water utterly transformed its performance such that by 1945 it was garnering enthusiastic praise from aircrews.

Defensive armament

The dorsal gunner had an excellent view from his well glazed turret atop the fuselage; by contrast the radio operator, who in most other contemporary designs was seated between the pilot and rear gunner, was consigned to a position within the rear fuselage of the aircraft known as 'the tunnel' or 'the cheap seats'. This crewmember was also expected man the ventral rear gun and utilize the Norden bombsight on level bombing missions. Both gun positions were virtually impossible to escape in an emergency.

Grumman TBF-1 Avenger

Weight: (Maximum takeoff) 8115kg (17895lb)
Dimensions: Length: 12.2m (40ft), Wingspan: 16.51m (54ft 2in), Height: 5m (16ft 5in)
Powerplant: One 1300kW (1700hp) Wright R-2600-8 Twin Cyclone 14-cylinder air-cooled radial piston engine
Speed: 447km/h (278mph)
Range: 1456km (905 miles)
Ceiling: 6900m (22600ft)
Crew: 3
Armament: One 7.62mm (0.3in) M1919 Browning machine gun fixed forward-firing in nose; one 12.7mm (0.5in) M2 Browning machine gun in rear turret, one 7.62mm (0.3in) M1919 Browning machine gun flexibly mounted in ventral position; up to 907kg (2000lb) bombload or one 907kg (2000lb) Mark XIII torpedo or Mark 24 acoustic homing torpedo in bomb bay

Radar

The Yagi-Uda antennae under each wing of this Avenger show that it was fitted with ASB radar, which could be used to detect and home onto air targets and surface vessels. This early radar was large and difficult to operate and was replaced by the X-band APS-4. The antenna used by the ASB system was developed, somewhat ironically, by two Japanese scientists Shintaro Uda and Hidetsugu Yagi, in 1926.

Cutaway key

1 Starboard elevator
2 Fabric-covered aileron construction
3 Elevator trim tab
4 Elevator horn balance
5 Tailplane construction
6 Rudder tab
7 Trim tab control jack
8 Tail navigation light
9 Fabric-covered rudder construction
10 Aerial cable rear mounting
11 Fin construction
12 Port elevator
13 Port tailplane
14 Elevator hinge controls
15 Tailplane support frames
16 Deck arrestor hook (lowered)
17 Arrestor hook guide rails
18 Rudder hinge control
19 Rear fuselage frames
20 Flush-riveted aluminium skin covering
21 Finroot fairing
22 Tailplane control cables
23 Arrestor hook retraction drive motor
24 Lifting tube
25 Rear fuselage frame and stringer construction
26 Tailwheel shock-absorber strut
27 Catapult 'holdback' shackle
28 Retractable tailwheel
29 Crew compartment rear bulkhead
30 Search flares
31 Parachute flare launch tube
32 Ventral gun turret
33 Ammunition magazine
34 Browning 7.62mm (0.3in) machinegun
35 Machine-gun mounting
36 Gun camera switch box
37 Crew door
38 Parachute stowage
39 Rear fuselage production break point
40 Spare coil stowage rack
41 Bombardier's side window
42 Upper turret spare ammunition magazines
43 Bombardier's folding seat
44 Gun turret mounting ring
45 Gun elevating mechanism
46 Ammunition feed chute
47 Browning 12.7mm (0.5in) machinegun
48 Upper rotating gun turret
49 Bulletproof windscreen
50 Gunner's armoured seat back
51 Aerial cable
52 Port wing, folded position
53 Canopy aft glazing
54 Emergency life raft stowage
55 Hydraulic reservoir
56 Radio communications equipment
57 ASB weapons aiming controller
58 Bomb release levers
59 Cabin heater duct
60 Aft end of bomb bay
61 Fixed wing, root construction
62 Wing fold joint line
63 Browning 12.7mm (0.5in)/ fixed machine-gun
64 Ammunition feed chute
65 Ammunition magazine (320 rounds)
66 Trailing-edge flap shroud construction
67 Lattice wing ribs

68 Starboard, fabric-covered aileron construction
69 Aileron hinge control
70 Aileron trim tab
71 Starboard wingtip
72 Starboard navigation light
73 Leading-edge ribs
74 Fixed leading-edge slot
75 ASB aerial

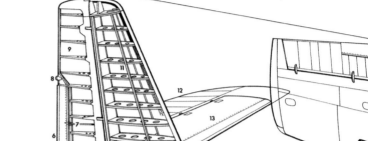

76 RT-5/APS-4 search radar pod
77 Radar mounting sway braces
78 Rocket-launching pylons
79 Jettisonable fuel tank
80 Main undercarriage wheel well
81 Sloping main spar
82 Wing fold hinge axis
83 Twin hydraulic folding jacks
84 Machine-gun blast tube
85 Starboard main fuel tank
86 Centre-section main spar
87 Oxygen bottle
88 Autopilot controls

89 Rear cockpit entry hatch
90 ASB equipment rack
91 Aerial mast
92 Roll-over crash pylon
93 Second cockpit control column provision
94 Propeller de-icing fluid tank
95 Seat-back armour
96 Headrest
97 Safety harness
98 Pilot's seat

99 Emergency hydraulic hand-pump
100 Centre main fuel tank
101 Fuel tank filler cap
102 Main undercarriage retraction jack
103 Wing fold locking cylinder
104 Machine-gun muzzle
105 Centre section leading-edge construction
106 Front fuselage frames
107 Rudder pedals
108 Back of instrument panel

109 Control column
110 Pilot's sliding entry hatch
111 Illuminated torpedo sight
112 Instrument panel shroud
113 Windscreen panels
114 Ring-and-bead gunsight
115 Gun camera
116 Port split trailing-edge flaps
117 Remote compass transmitter

TBM-1C Avenger

118 Aileron control rods
119 Aileron hinge control
120 Fabric-covered port aileron
121 Aileron trim tab
122 Formation light
123 Pitot tube
124 Port navigation light
125 Fixed leading-edge slot
126 Wing 'tie-down' shackle
127 ASB aerial mounting
128 Retractable landing lamp
129 Red, white and green approach lights
130 Port ASB aerial
131 Ground attack rockets
132 Oil tank filler cap

133 Engine oil tank 49 litres (13 US gal)
134 Engine compartment bulkhead
135 Engine mounting struts
136 Cowling air exit flap
137 Twin carburettors
138 Carburettor air trunking
139 Wright-cyclone, 14-cylinder, two-row radial engine
140 Carburettor air intake
141 Propeller governor
142 Reduction gearbox
143 Hamilton Standard three-bladed propeller
144 Engine cooling intake
145 Engine cowlings
146 Cowling air flap control lever
147 Lower cowling air flap

148 Batteries
149 Starboard exhaust pipe
150 Oil cooler
151 Oil cooler air exit flap
152 Bomb release shackle
153 227kg (500lb) bombs
154 Bomb bay door construction
155 Bomb doors (open)

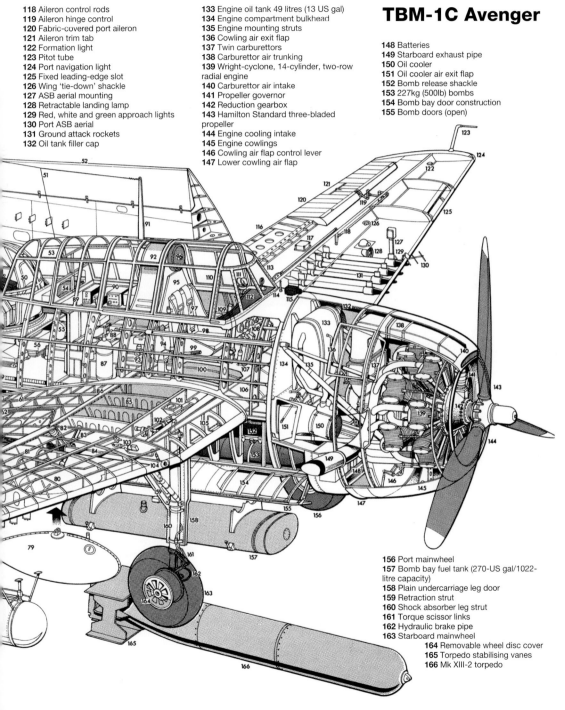

156 Port mainwheel
157 Bomb bay fuel tank (270-US gal/1022-litre capacity)
158 Plain undercarriage leg door
159 Retraction strut
160 Shock absorber leg strut
161 Torque scissor links
162 Hydraulic brake pipe
163 Starboard mainwheel
164 Removable wheel disc cover
165 Torpedo stabilising vanes
166 Mk XIII-2 torpedo

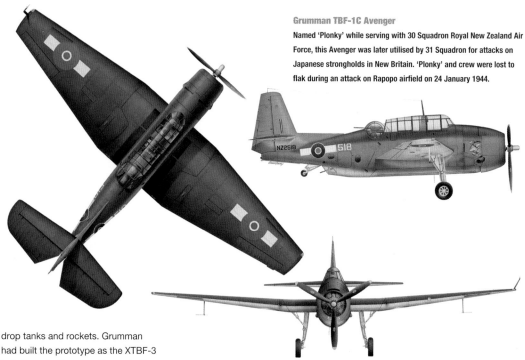

Grumman TBF-1C Avenger

Named 'Plonky' while serving with 30 Squadron Royal New Zealand Air Force, this Avenger was later utilised by 31 Squadron for attacks on Japanese strongholds in New Britain. 'Plonky' and crew were lost to flak during an attack on Rapopo airfield on 24 January 1944.

drop tanks and rockets. Grumman had built the prototype as the XTBF-3 but all production aircraft were built by General Motors. The final major version to enter service before the end of the war was the TBM-3E, a lightened version that was 1179kg (2600lb) lighter than TBM-3, most of which was accounted for by deleting the ventral gun and its ammunition supply.

Hunter/killer system

As the war progressed the Avenger was used in a greater variety of roles than torpedo bombing, with ever more attacks being made on shore targets in support of the island-hopping campaign through the Pacific. However, the aircraft also became the most successful carrier based anti-submarine aircraft of the war and was responsible for sinking 30 submarines over the course of the conflict, mostly by aircraft flown off escort carriers attached to Atlantic convoys. A specialized subtype, the TBF-1D, or TBM-1D

depending on where it was built, was produced with an ASD-1 radar set in a radome on the starboard wing. This in turn led to the development of the hunter/killer system where a sensor-equipped TBM-3W would locate the submarine and the heavily armed TBM-3S would engage it. Developed during the war, the system was not deployed in time to see action, though the hunter/killer combination was further developed post-war in the form of the Grumman AF-2W and AF-2S Guardian.

After VJ Day the Avenger served on into the early 1960s, primarily as an ASW and AEW asset with several navies. In civilian hands it served for many years more as a firefighting aircraft, with the final Avenger serving in this role being retired by Forest Protection Ltd of New Brunswick in 2012.

Grumman TBF-1 Avenger

Weight: (Maximum takeoff) 8115kg (17895lb)

Dimensions: Length: 12.2m (40ft), Wingspan: 16.51m (54ft 2in), Height: 5m (16ft 5in)

Powerplant: One 1300kW (1700hp) Wright R-2600-8 Twin Cyclone 14-cylinder air-cooled radial piston engine

Speed: 447km/h (278mph)

Range: 1456km (905 miles)

Ceiling: 6900m (22600ft)

Crew: 3

Armament: One 7.62mm (0.3in) M1919 Browning machine gun fixed forward-firing in nose; one 12.7mm (0.5in) M2 Browning machine gun in rear turret, one 7.62mm (0.3in) M1919 Browning machine gun flexibly mounted in ventral position; up to 907kg (2000lb) bombload or one 907kg (2000lb) Mark XIII torpedo or Mark 24 acoustic homing torpedo in bomb bay

de Havilland Sea Mosquito

A naval version of de Havilland's formidable Mosquito, the Sea Mosquito became the first British twin-engine aircraft to land on an aircraft carrier.

de Havilland Sea Mosquito TR Mk.33

The Sea Mosquito was the result of a bold scheme to take the RAF's most successful medium bomber to sea. Although it was proved that the Mosquito could land on a carrier, it was acknowledged to be very difficult. This 771 Squadron example was based at Lee-on-Solent in 1948.

The radical de Havilland Mosquito, an aircraft of wooden construction initially schemed as a bomber fast enough to dispense with defensive armament but also employed as a reconnaissance, anti-shipping, night fighter and fighter-bomber aircraft, had seen spectacularly successful service with the RAF since 1941. Naval interest resulted in specification N.I 5/44 being written specifically to cover a navalized Mosquito variant. Changes included the fitting of folding wings, arrestor hook, thimble nose radar installation, Merlin 25 engines with four-bladed propellers and a new oleo-pneumatic landing gear in place of rubber-in-compression units of the standard Mosquito. The new version was designated the Sea Mosquito TR Mk.33.

First carrier landing

During early 1944, test pilot Eric Brown undertook carrier trials with the first navalized Mosquito, an FB.VI that had been modified to TR Mk.33 standard to test the feasibility of operating such a large aircraft at sea. On 25 March Brown made the first carrier landing of a twin-engine British aircraft when he successfully landed on HMS *Indefatigable*. An order for 100 TR Mk.33s was placed but in the event only 50 production aircraft were constructed by de Havilland, the first flying in November 1945. A mere six examples were built of an improved variant, the TR Mk 37, which featured the British ASV Mk.XIII radar in an enlarged radome replacing the American AN/APS-6 unit of the TR Mk.33.

The production aircraft ultimately never served at sea and were used to replace the Royal Navy's shore-based Mosquito FB.VI anti-shipping aircraft of 811 squadron stationed at RNAS Brawdy in South Wales, serving until that unit's disbandment in July 1947.

de Havilland TR.33 Sea Mosquito

Weight: (Maximum takeoff) 9979kg (22,000lb)

Dimensions: Length: 12.55m (41ft 7in), Wingspan: 16.52m (54ft 2in), Height: 5.3m (17ft 5in)

Powerplant: 2kW (1635hp) Rolls-Royce Merlin 25 V-12 liquid-cooled piston engines

Speed: 612km/h (380mph)

Range: 1840km (1143 miles)

Ceiling: 12,000m (39,370ft)

Crew: 2

Armament: Four 20mm Hispano cannon fixed forward firing under nose; one 1670lb torpedo under fuselage or up to 1361kg (3000lb) bombload or eight 27kg (60lb) rockets underwing

Martin AM-1 Mauler

The huge Mauler was developed at the end of World War II as a result of changing ideas regarding Naval attack aircraft. Its career was short but it carved a niche in aviation history due to its weight-lifting capability.

By 1943 it was becoming clear that the roles of torpedo and dive bomber could be combined in one, single-seat airframe rather than the multi-crew aircraft that had so far been the norm for these tasks. The US Navy accordingly invited proposals for a single-seat, multi-purpose attack aircraft. Somewhat ironically, Martin's proposal was intended as a relatively simple low-risk backup to the Curtiss XBTC which had been selected to replace the SB2C Helldiver. Martin were specifically requested to design an 'unexperimental' airframe to utilize the new Pratt & Whitney R-4360 Wasp Major that had been specified for both aircraft. The XBTC remained a prototype but the Martin design, which had made its first flight on 26 August 1944, went into production when an order for 750 AM-1 Maulers was placed in January 1945.

Structural integrity

Unfortunately, all was not entirely well with the Mauler. Aerodynamic problems with the cowling, fin and rudder all surfaced during testing as well as structural issues with the rear fuselage.

During carrier trials one aircraft broke in half as a result of a heavy landing. The issues were corrected but doubts lingered about the aircraft's strength. It was only during 1949 that units completed carrier qualifications, the first being VA-17A, and took the Mauler to sea. In March of the same year an AM-1 flew with three torpedoes of 998kg (2200lb) each, 12 113kg (250lb) bombs as well as its four 20mm (0.79in) guns and their ammunition, equating to a total ordnance load of 4830kg (10,648lb), which remains an unofficial record for a single piston engine-powered aircraft. In service the AM-1 garnered respect for its load carrying ability, earning the nickname 'Able Mabel' as a result, although maintenance crews would allegedly joke that AM actually stood for 'Awful Monster' due to its mechanical unreliability, particularly the hydraulic system. Pilots disliked its deck landing characteristics and its heavy controls, much preferring the smaller, simpler and more reliable Skyraider. All Maulers were shore-based by 1950 and withdrawn during 1953.

Martin AM-1 Mauler

An undeniably impressive aircraft, the Mauler was intended to be a relatively simple 'low-risk' option for a single-seat attack aircraft but was itself sidelined by an even simpler aircraft in the form of the Skyraider. This reserve AM-1 was based at Glenview Naval Air Station in the early 1950s.

Martin AM-1 Mauler

Weight: (Maximum takeoff) 11700kg (25794lb)

Dimensions: Length: 12.57m (41ft 3in), Wingspan: 15.24m (50ft), Height: 5.13m (16ft 10in)

Powerplant: One 2200kW (3000hp) Pratt & Whitney R-4360 Wasp Major 28-cylinder air-cooled radial piston engine

Speed: 538km/h (334mph)

Range: 2452km (1524 miles)

Ceiling: 8200m (27,000ft)

Crew: 1

Armament: Four 20mm (0.79in) T-31 cannon fixed forward-firing in wings; up to 4830kg (10,648lb) bombload on 15 external hardpoints

Douglas AD-1 Skyraider

One of the most important aircraft to emerge as a result of World War II, yet destined to play no part in it, the Skyraider's contribution to the wars in Korea and Vietnam became near-legendary.

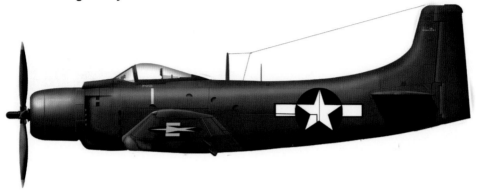

In a bid to replace both the SBD Dauntless and Curtiss SB2C Helldiver with one airframe Ed Heineman at Douglas had designed the XSB2D-1 'Dauntless II', first flown in April 1943 featuring a tricycle undercarriage, bomb bay and wing racks for up to 1900kg (4200lb) of bombs or one torpedo. Defensive armament consisted of two wing-mounted cannon and two remote-controlled turrets, each with two 12.7mm (0.5in) machine guns.

Although this aircraft was fast, it was also very heavy and prohibitively complex, and the Navy requested a single-seat version in line with its current thinking on attack aircraft. In single-seat form the new aircraft could now carry two torpedoes as well as more fuel and armour and production was ordered as the BTD-1 Destroyer. Unfortunately, increased weight meant the BTD had worse performance than the XSB2D-1 and production was cancelled after only 28 examples had been built. Seeking to reverse the trend for ever more complex and heavy aircraft, Heineman subjected the BTD

to a major weight-saving programme that saw such features as the internal bomb bay and tricycle undercarriage discarded in the ruthless quest for as low an empty weight as possible. First flown on 18 March 1945, the XBT2D-1 was evaluated at the Naval Air Test Center in April and ordered into production as the AD-1 Skyraider. First production aircraft were delivered to VA-19A in December 1946.

Effective service

In service the aircraft proved popular and effective. The aircraft remained in production until 1957 by which time it seemed an anachronism in an increasingly jet-dominated world, but over Korea and Vietnam its slow speed accuracy, resilience to ground fire and 10-hour endurance exceeded the abilities of other attack aircraft. The Skyraider would go on to serve with the USAAF and VPAF (Vietnam People's Air Force) in large numbers as well as with the air arms of eight other nations, the last being retired by Gabon in 1985.

Douglas XBT2D-1 Skyraider

Designer Ed Heineman worked out that for every 45kg (100lb) of weight lost, combat radius increased by 35km (22 miles). A rigorous weight reduction programme transformed the somewhat humdrum initial XBT2D-1 design into the prototype of the superlative Skyraider, pictured here.

Douglas AD-1 Skyraider

Weight: (Maximum takeoff) 8178kg (18029lb)

Dimensions: Length: 12m (39ft 3in), Wingspan: 15.24m (50ft), Height: 4.8m (17ft 8in)

Powerplant: One 1865kW (2500hp) Wright R-3350-24W Duplex Cyclone 18-cylinder air-cooled radial piston engine

Speed: 517km/h (321mph)

Range: 2500km (1553 miles)

Ceiling: 7925m (26000ft)

Crew: 1

Armament: Two (later four) 20mm (0.787in) AN/M3 cannon fixed forward firing in wings; bombload up to 3629kg (8000lb)

SEAPLANES, FLYING BOATS & HELICOPTERS

Much of the aviation requirements of the Allied navies during World War II centered around searching out the enemy, correcting naval gunfire (a role which was increasingly rendered obsolete by radar), and such vital but unsung tasks as communications with shore and air sea rescue. Aircraft designed for these roles were often present on capital ships as well as aboard aircraft carriers.

This chapter includes the following aircraft:

- Supermarine Walrus
- Curtiss SO3C Seamew
- Curtiss SOC Seagull
- Sikorsky HNS-1
- Loire 130
- Curtiss S4C Seahawk
- North American SNJ
- Grumman J2F Duck
- Latécoère 298
- Fairey Seafox
- Vought OS2U Kingfisher
- Supermarine Sea Otter

USS *Biloxi,* catapults a Curtiss SO3C Seamew while on its shakedown cruise, circa October 1943. Catapult operations aboard capital ships diminished over the course of the war and were effectively brought to an end by the development of the helicopter in the immediate post-war period.

Supermarine Walrus

Designed for use on warship catapults, the elderly but versatile Walrus ultimately made its greatest contribution to the Allied war effort as an Air-Sea Rescue aircraft.

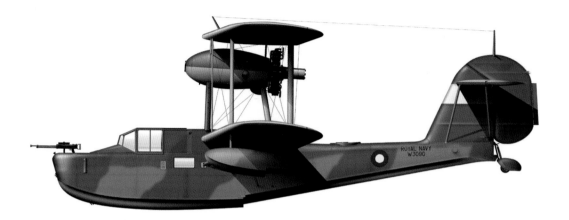

The Walrus stemmed from an Australian requirement calling for a successor to their 1921 vintage Supermarine Seagull III flying boats. Supermarine's chief designer R.J. Mitchell had already designed an amphibian flying boat that fitted the Australian specification called the Seagull V and the RAAF duly ordered a prototype from the firm. Supermarine were extremely busy in the early 1930s, with the Seagull V considered a low priority and prototype construction, despite being started in 1930, was severely delayed. The aircraft eventually made its first flight on 21 June 1933, but only after pressure had been put on Supermarine from the Australian High Commission in London.

British orders

A mere five days after its first flight the Seagull V appeared at an air display at Hendon where test pilot J.F. 'Mutt' Summers astonished the

Supermarine Walrus Mk.I

Serving with 1700 squadron aboard the escort carrier HMS *Ameer* with the British Pacific Fleet in July 1945, W3090 was one of the metal-hulled Mk.Is. The aircraft is pictured as it appeared on 8 July 1945 when it rescued a downed Hellcat pilot a mere 180 metres (200 yards) off the Japanese held coast.

crowd (including designer Mitchell) by performing a loop in the new flying boat. Trials revealed that the Seagull V was able to operate from a remarkably rough sea and was fully capable of catapult launches from battleships and cruisers. An Australian order for 24 was placed in January 1935 and the RAF, impressed with the aircraft's performance during its trials, ordered 12 in May, specifying that the British name would be Walrus. Further orders were rapidly placed and Supermarine, fully committed to Spitfire production, constructed a new factory a few miles from its main Woolston factory to produce the Walrus. Even this could

Supermarine Walrus Mk.I

Weight: (Maximum takeoff) 8050kg (3651lb)
Dimensions: Length: 11.46m (37ft 7in), Wingspan: 13.97m (45ft 10in), Height: 4.65m (15ft 3in)
Powerplant: One 560kW (750hp) Bristol Pegasus VI nine-cylinder air-cooled radial piston engine
Speed: 217km/h (135mph)
Range: 970km (600 miles)
Ceiling: 5600m (18,500ft)
Crew: 4
Armament: One 7.7mm (0.303in) Vickers K machine gun flexibly mounted in nose position, one 7.7mm (0.303in) Vickers K machine gun flexibly mounted in dorsal position; up to 450kg (600lb) bombload

not keep up with demand and most Walruses were built under licence by Saunders-Roe on the Isle of Wight.

Despite its biplane configuration, the Walrus was quite an advanced aircraft for its era, being the first British military aircraft to combine the features of retractable undercarriage, a fully enclosed cockpit and a metal fuselage in the same airframe. The hull was initially of anodized alloy construction although the Mk.II version substituted this for an all-wood hull due to wartime shortages of light alloys. A curious feature of the aircraft was that the entire engine nacelle assembly was angled three degrees to the right to counteract the torque of the propeller.

Submarine patrol

Initially operated by catapult flights, Walruses would serve on 59 British Commonwealth capital ships, beginning with the prototype, K4747, which was assigned to the Battleship HMS *Nelson* after the completion of trials. The primary task for Royal Navy Walruses assigned to cruisers and battleships was expected to be gunnery spotting in naval actions,

however the Walrus would perform this function only twice, at the battles of Cape Spartivento and Cape Matapan. The main tasks carried out by the Walrus from warships was patrolling for submarines and enemy shipping and Walruses would begin to receive ASV radar as early as March 1941 to assist in this task.

Improvements in radar equipment saw the use of aircraft aboard ships diminish by 1943, but the Walrus continued to serve at sea for the duration of the war aboard aircraft carriers as both an air-sea rescue and communications aircraft. Despite not being fitted with an arrestor hook, the very low landing speed of the Walrus meant it could operate perfectly well without one from a carrier deck.

However, the majority of the Walrus's usage was shore based with the RAF as an air-sea rescue aircraft, being responsible for saving around 1000 aircrew during the course of the war. After the end of hostilities the Walrus saw service with several navies, the last operating, as originally intended, as a catapult aircraft on the Argentine cruiser *La Argentina* as late as 1958.

This Walrus is being recovered by a Royal Navy cruiser (either HMS *York* or *Exeter*) and is about to be hoisted aboard by crane. The crewman standing on the lower wing has climbed down after attaching the line to the centre section above the top wing, a precarious operation, even in calm weather.

Curtiss SOC Seagull

The SOC Seagull was a typical mid-1930s catapult-launched floatplane scout. The poor performance of its intended successor saw it returned to service and it fulfilled this role until the end of the conflict.

First flying in April 1934, the Curtiss SOC entered service in November 1935 aboard the light cruiser USS *Marblehead* and by 1939 had been universally adopted across the fleet, replacing the Vought O2U Corsair aboard cruisers and battleships. The SOC was first flown with a single large float containing a retractable undercarriage but this feature was abandoned and provision was made on production aircraft to remove the float and fit a fixed undercarriage for land operations. After building 135 SOC-1s, 40 SOC-2s were constructed as wheeled aircraft only with a slightly more powerful Wasp engine before it too was supplanted by the SOC-3 in which the interchangeable undercarriage was reinstated, 83 of which were built.

Coast Guard role

After 1941 several SOC-2s and 3s were fitted with a hook for carrier operations and re-designated SOC-2A

and 3A. Three of a final SOC-4 model were built to a Coast Guard search and rescue contract but these were taken over by the Navy and modified to SOC-3A standard. In addition to the aircraft built by Curtiss, a further 64 SOC-3 equivalent aircraft were built by the Naval Aircraft Factory as the SON-1.

During 1941 the name Seagull was adopted for the SOC and after the US entered the war the aircraft saw action in all theatres in which the US Navy participated. As it was gradually supplanted by the Vought OS2U Kingfisher on larger ships, the Seagull transferred to the training role. However, the shortcomings of the Curtiss SO3C Seamew that had been expressly designed to replace it saw the Seagull reinstated aboard catapult-equipped vessels too small to handle the Vought OS2U Kingfisher during 1943.

Curtiss SOC-1 Seagull

Assigned to the heavy cruiser USS *Tuscaloosa*, this Seagull is depicted as it appeared during 1943, when *Tuscaloosa* was part of the escort for the RMS *Queen Mary* conveying Winston Churchill to New York. *Tuscaloosa* relinquished her Seagulls just before the Normandy landings in June 1944.

Curtiss SOC-1 Seagull

Weight: (Maximum takeoff) 2466kg (5437lb)
Dimensions: Length: 9.58m (31ft 5in), Wingspan: 10.97m (36ft), Height: 4.5m (14ft 9in)
Powerplant: One 450kW (600hp) Pratt & Whitney R-1340-18 Wasp nine-cylinder, air-cooled, radial piston engine
Speed: 266km/h (165mph)
Range: 1086km (675 miles)
Ceiling: 4500m (14,900ft)
Crew: 2
Armament: One 7.62mm (0.3in) Browning M2/AN machine gun fixed forward-firing in cowling, one 7.62mm (0.3in) Browning M2/AN machine gun flexibly mounted in rear cockpit; up to 295kg (650lb) bombload

Loire 130

Described as 'one of the ugliest aircraft ever built', the squat Loire 130 delivered reliable service over much of the globe for the duration of the war and beyond.

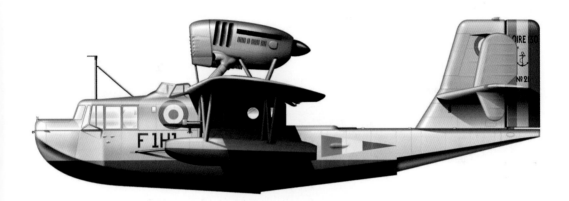

Designed for a broadly similar role as the Supermarine Walrus, the Loire 130 first flew on 19 November 1934, but stability problems proved difficult to resolve and an initial production order was only placed in August 1936. Aircraft began to be received by operational units during 1938 and not all aircraft on order had been completed by the French Armistice of June 1940. Production aircraft were produced in two series, the Loire 130M '*Metropole*' intended for use in France and the 130C '*Coloniale*' for service in France's overseas territories. The latter was fitted with a larger radiator and strengthened structure to permit shallow dive bombing. In contrast to the Walrus, the pilot of the Loire 130 sat in an open cockpit but the other members of the crew had enclosed positions in the spacious cabin. An additional four passengers could be carried by the aircraft if required.

Slow speed

During 1939 and 40 the Loire 130 became the standard naval catapult

aircraft aboard all large French capital ships as well as serving aboard the seaplane tender *Commandante Teste*. Various *Armee de l'Air* units also formed on the Loire 130 in the French Antilles, West Africa, the Middle East and French Indochina.

In service

In service the Loire 130 performed gunnery ranging, coastal patrol, convoy escort and liaison and while very slow, its endurance of up to seven and a half hours was impressive and useful. After the armistice with Germany, several examples were taken into German service and production continued for Vichy French requirements. The Loire performed reconnaissance work during the Franco–Thai war of October 1940 to January 1941, but in November 1942 catapult equipment was removed from French warships and all Loire 130s were henceforth shore-based for the remainder of their service lives. The last example was retired by *Escadrille* 8.S in Indochina in late 1949.

Loire 130

Although it could hardly be described as sleek, the Loire 130 enjoyed a long and successful career. This example was attached to *Flotille* F1H based at Karouba in Tunisia during May 1940.

Loire 130

Weight: (Maximum takeoff) 3500kg (7716lb)
Dimensions: Length: 11.3m (37ft 1in), Wingspan: 16m (52ft 6in), Height: 3.85m (12ft 8in)
Powerplant: One 540kW (720hp) Hispano-Suiza 12Xirs V-12 liquid-cooled piston engine
Speed: 220km/h (137mph)
Range: 1100km (634 miles)
Ceiling: 6000m (19,685ft)
Crew: 3
Armament: One 7.5mm (0.295in) Darne machine gun fixed forward-firing in bow, one 7.5mm (0.295in) Darne machine gun flexibly mounted in dorsal position; up to 150kg (330lb) bombload on external racks on forward hull

North American SNJ Texan

Of all the fighting powers of World War II, the US was unique in developing a deck-landing training aircraft. This aircraft was the North American SNJ, a navalized version of the ubiquitous T-6.

The origin of the hugely successful North American series of monoplane trainers was the NA-16 prototype that first flew on 1 April 1935, initially with an open cockpit and Wright R-975 engine. Subsequently developed into a bewildering number of variants, the first examples of this diverse family ordered for the US Navy were 40 of the NJ-1, powered by the Pratt & Whitney R-1340 Wasp and featuring a fixed undercarriage. The aircraft was subsequently developed with retractable undercarriage and small numbers of the SNJ-1 were ordered, equivalent to the British Harvard I and the SNJ-2 with a different Wasp engine. The first carrier-capable variant was the SNJ-3C, 12 of which were modified from standard SNJ-3s.

Korean War

The first truly mass-produced versions were the SNJ-4, 1240 examples of which were built that featured an airframe featuring more steel and wood to minimize the use of strategic light alloys, and the 1573 SNJ-5s

that was basically identical but fitted with a 24-volt electrical system. When fitted with an arrestor hook the aircraft became the SNJ-4C and 5C respectively. These two aircraft were the standard trainers of naval aviators throughout the war and were used to instruct students in everything from formation and instrument flying to the challenging art of deck landing. So successful was the SNJ in this role that it persisted as the standard USN deck-landing trainer well into the 1950s. Indeed, an absence of any successor saw many mothballed SNJs returned to service when the Korean War prompted an increased need for new naval aviators.

The aircraft also played a part in the development of the carrier itself as an SNJ was the first aircraft to land and take off from the first US angled-deck carrier the USS *Antietam* in 1953. In total the T-6/SNJ series served in the air forces of over 60 nations, the final examples being retired by the South African Air Force in 1995.

North American SNJ-3

Depicted as it appeared in the last few months before the US entered the war, this SNJ-3 sports the chrome yellow wing surfaces, intended to aid locating the aircraft in the event it was forced down at sea. These were standard for USN aircraft throughout the late 1920s and 1930s.

North American SNJ-5C Texan

Weight: (Maximum takeoff) 2495kg (5500lb)

Dimensions: Length: 8.8m (29ft), Wingspan: 12.9m (42ft), Height: 3.5m (11ft 9in)

Powerplant: One 410kW (550hp) Pratt & Whitney R-1340-AN1 Wasp seven-cylinder air-cooled radial piston engine

Speed: 331km/h (205mph)

Range: 1200km (750 miles)

Ceiling: 6560m (21,500ft)

Crew: 2

Armament: One 7.62mm (0.3in) M1919 Browning machine gun fixed, forward firing in forward fuselage, one 7.62mm (0.3in) M1919 Browning machine gun fixed forward firing in starboard wing, one 7.62mm (0.3in) M1919 Browning machine gun flexibly mounted in rear cockpit

Grumman J2F Duck

The portly, amphibious Grumman JF and J2F Duck operated as a general utility aircraft performing various unglamorous but vital roles from shore bases and aboard carriers.

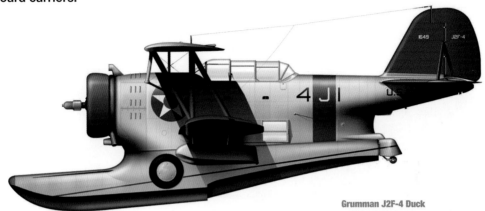

Grumman J2F-4 Duck
Built by Grumman in 1939, J2F-4 Duck, Bureau number 1649, was stationed at Pearl Harbor and survived the Japanese attack on 7 December 1941. Struck off USN charge in 1947, it was used for a time to transport fish in the Bahamas before being restored and is currently the only airworthy Grumman-built Duck worldwide.

Grumman developed the JF-1 as a carrier-based aircraft to perform such tasks as communication flights between ship and shore, short range reconnaissance, air-sea rescue and casualty evacuation. It first flew on 24 April 1933 and although only 48 were built they served aboard all the major fleet carriers of the US Navy, gaining the nickname 'Duck', as well as with the US Coast Guard and Argentine Navy. Grumman developed the design and although the changes were relatively modest the aircraft received the new designation of J2F, although it also inherited the 'Duck' nickname, which became official when the USN decided on a naming policy for all its aircraft.

Marine Corps

The J2F, first flown on 2 April 1935, gained a Wright Cyclone of greater power than the Twin Wasp then fitted to the JF but in most respects the aircraft differed little from its predecessor. The standard aircraft featured tandem

cockpits for the pilot and navigator with a cabin inside the hull for two passengers or a stretcher. This cabin was also used for radio equipment and cameras for the photographic reconnaissance role. Most examples possessed no gun armament, but a batch of 21 J2F-2s were supplied to the Marine Corps with nose and dorsal guns and underwing bomb racks to fly armed Neutrality Patrols over the Caribbean. Around 20 were painted dark blue and silver and fitted out for VIPs such as the Naval Air Attaché as so-called 'Admiral's barges'.

Both the J2F-4 and later models were equipped with target towing gear, further increasing the aircraft's usefulness, and J2Fs were ultimately flown by the USAAF (as the OA-12) and US Coast Guard as well as the Navy and Marine Corps.

The final variant was the J2F-6 that was developed and built by Columbia Aircraft, who had taken over production due to pressure of other work at Grumman, and this model was able to

undertake short range anti-submarine missions in addition to the more mundane tasks usually associated with the Duck. In total, 584 were built and served long into the post-war era, the last being retired by Peru in 1964.

Grumman J2F-6

Weight: (Maximum takeoff) 3493kg (7700lb)
Dimensions: Length: 10.36m (34ft), Wingspan: 11.89m (39ft), Height: 4.24m (13ft 11in)
Powerplant: One 670kW (900hp) Wright R-1820-54 Cyclone 9-cylinder, air-cooled, radial piston engine
Speed: 310km/h (190mph)
Range: 1260km (780 miles)
Ceiling: 6100m (20,000ft)
Crew: 2
Armament: One 7.62mm (0.3in) Browning M1919 machine gun flexibly mounted in rear cockpit; up to 295kg (650lb) bombload

Latécoère 298

The sturdy and manoeuvrable Latécoère 298 multipurpose floatplane was intended to operate from coastal bases and the seaplane tender *Commandante Teste*. Its excellent qualities saw it serve throughout the war on both sides of the conflict.

Despite first flying on 8 May 1936, a relatively leisurely development and crew training period saw the Latécoère 298 only enter service with operational units in January 1939. The aircraft was intended to perform as a level or dive bomber, reconnaissance aircraft or torpedo bomber and was initially produced in two series: the standard Laté 298A and the Laté 298B with folding outer wing panels for operations from the *Commandante Teste*. France was unique among European nations in fielding a seaplane tender in the late 1930s and assigned two Laté 298B squadrons to her, HB1 and HB2.

French armistice

After the outbreak of war, the Latécoères undertook anti-shipping patrols but a lack of targets saw them switched to operations against invading German land forces during May and June 1940 before being transferred to the Mediterranean to briefly fight against Italian naval forces until the French armistice brought an end to

combat operations. By this time 110 Latécoère 298s had been built, later examples being of the improved 298D variant, and a further 20 would be constructed by the Vichy regime. Most of the surviving aircraft flew maritime patrol missions along the North African coast but one Latécoère defected to Malta in July 1940 and was subsequently flown in RAF markings for reconnaissance and leaflet dropping.

Following the Allied victory in Operation Torch the Latécoère 298s in Africa continued to fly maritime patrol under Allied control. Of those remaining in Vichy France when Germany occupied the nation in November 1942, one was tested with German equipment as a prelude to conversion of the remaining 45 for Luftwaffe use but this plan was abandoned when Operation Dragoon saw the Allies invade Southern France.

After the war the Latécoère 298 was utilized by the *Aéronautique Naval* as a trainer. The final example, serving with *Escadrille* 53.S, was withdrawn during 1951.

Latécoère 298B

This Laté was on the strength of *Escadrille* HB1, one of two squadrons nominally assigned to the seaplane carrier *Commandante Teste*. HB1's aircraft were based at Karouba, Tunisia, when Italy attacked French military assets in the Mediterranean during June 1940.

Latécoère 298D

Weight: (Maximum takeoff) 4533kg (9994lb)
Dimensions: Length: 12.56m (41ft 2in), Wingspan: 15.5m (50ft 10in), Height: 5.25m (17ft 3in)
Powerplant: One 660kW (880hp) Hispano-Suiza 12Ycrs V-12 liquid-cooled piston engine
Speed: 295km/h (183mph)
Range: 1000km (620 miles)
Ceiling: 5500m (18,000ft)
Crew: 3
Armament: Two 7.5mm (0.295in) Darne machine guns fixed forward-firing in wings, one 7.5mm (0.295in) Darne machine gun flexibly mounted in rear cockpit; up to 680kg (1500lb) bombload or one 680kg (1500lb) torpedo

Fairey Seafox

The Fairey Seafox was only built in small numbers and was compromised by its overcomplex and maintenance-heavy engine, but participated in one of the most dramatic naval battles during the first year of the war.

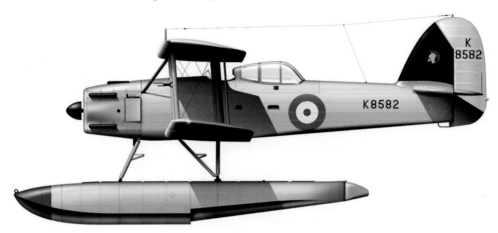

A generally conventional floatplane, the Seafox first flew on 27 May 1936, demonstrating pleasant handling, although it was considered somewhat underpowered when committed to service. The observer had the unusual luxury, for a British aircraft of this era, of a fully enclosed cockpit, which could be opened forwards to provide a windbreak, facilitating usage of the rear gun. The pilot meanwhile was seated in an open cockpit, the justification for this being that he required an unrestricted view for catapult operations. Performance was modest but acceptable and an order for 64 production aircraft was placed in addition to the two prototypes.

Catapult tests took place aboard the cruiser HMS *Neptune*. After the first entered service during April 1937, the aircraft was deployed aboard vessels that were too small to handle the more commonplace Supermarine Walrus or Fairey Swordfish floatplane. In operational use the greatest issue

with the Seafox was its air-cooled Napier Rapier engine, a complex unit with 16 cylinders arranged in four banks of four. While this resulted in an impressively compact engine with a much smaller frontal area than an equivalent radial engine, the rearmost cylinders tended to overheat and the engine was difficult to maintain. Nonetheless, the Seafox was widely used and served into 1943.

Battle of the River Plate

The Seafox's greatest moment came when it spotted for the guns of HMS *Ajax* during the Battle of the River Plate during which the German battleship *Graf Spee* was pursued to Montevideo in neutral Uruguay, where it was reconnoitred by the Seafox before being scuttled. This was the first instance in which an aircraft spotted for ship's guns in battle during World War II as well as being one of the last naval engagements fought without the benefit of radar.

Fairey Seafox

K8582 was one of two Seafoxes carried by the cruiser HMS *Ajax* and is seen here in its pre-war colour scheme with black fin and badge depicting an Ancient Greek helmet. K8582 was damaged before the Battle of the River Plate and thus sister aircraft K8591 performed gun spotting for *Ajax* during this historic action.

Fairey Seafox

Weight: (Maximum takeoff) 2458kg (5420lb)

Dimensions: Length: 10.19m (33ft 5in), Wingspan: 12m (40ft), Height: 3.71m (12ft 2in)

Powerplant: One 295kW (395hp) Napier Rapier VI H-16 air-cooled piston engine

Speed: 200km/h (124mph)

Range: 710km (440 miles)

Ceiling: 3000m (9700ft)

Crew: 2

Armament: One 7.7mm (0.303in) Vickers K machine gun flexibly mounted in rear cockpit; up to 163kg (360lb) bombload

---

Vought OS2U Kingfisher

The US Navy's standard shipboard floatplane for the majority of the war, the unassuming OS2U Kingfisher proved reliable and versatile and served for considerably longer than had been planned.

When it entered service in August 1940, the Vought OS2U was the first catapult-launched monoplane to be operated by the US Navy. Designed by Rex Beisel, who was also responsible for the F4U Corsair, the OS2U was the first production aircraft to be constructed using spot welding, a process Vought had developed in conjunction with the Naval Aircraft Factory, which would build 300 examples of the OS2N. It made its maiden flight on 1 March 1938.

Like the SOC it partially replaced, the Kingfisher, as it was named during 1941, featured interchangeable float or

Vought OS2U Kingfisher

Australia received several Kingfishers originally intended for use by the Netherlands East Indies, putting them into RAAF service during late 1942 and early 1943. A48-18 flew initially with the Seaplane Training Flight, later 3 OTU, and 107 Sqn, with whom it was coded JE-T.

LEFT & OPPOSITE: A Vought OS2U Kingfisher floatplane, of Observation Squadron One (VO-1), being towed on a mat by USS *Arizona* (BB-39), while being recovered after a flight in the Hawaiian Operating area, 6 September 1941. The pilot was Lieutenant-Commander Welton D. Rowley, commanding officer of VO-1. To the rear, Radioman 2nd Class E.L. Higley (pictured opposite), prepares to go out on the plane's wing to hook up the aircraft to the battleship's crane for recovery.

wheeled undercarriage and operated from both catapult-equipped ships and shore bases throughout its career. The Kingfisher quickly became the standard aircraft operating in the gunnery spotting observation and air sea rescue role from the US Navy's capital ships, battleships normally carrying three aircraft, although the powerful new *Iowa* class battleships featured four OS2Us apiece when they were commissioned.

Inshore Patrol Squadrons

The OS2U also exclusively equipped the Inshore Patrol Squadrons engaged in anti-submarine warfare in coastal waters. In service the OS2U was popular, proving robust and dependable. Notable operations included one example that rescued the World War I ace Eddie Rickenbacker

and three other survivors of a B-17 crash after 24 days at sea in a dinghy. Unable to take off with this many passengers and loath to leave any behind for fear they would not later be found, the Kingfisher pilot taxied 64km (40 miles) to rendezvous with a PT boat with the rescued men sitting on the wings.

By late 1944, the high-performance Curtiss SC Seahawk began to replace the OS2U but several remained on warships until VJ Day. Many of the 1519 OS2Us constructed were exported through lend-lease channels to fellow combatants – the British Royal Navy received 100 Kingfisher Mk.Is in place of the disappointing Curtiss Seamew, serving with several squadrons and aboard two light cruisers. Australia, Cuba, Chile, Mexico, the USSR and Uruguay all received O2SUs, with at

least one Cuban example surviving to be flown as a ground attack machine by Fidel Castro's forces during the revolution of 1959.

Vought OS2U-3 Kingfisher

Weight: (Maximum takeoff) 2722kg (6000lb)
Dimensions: Length: 10.24m (33ft 7in), Wingspan: 10.94m (35ft 11in), Height: 4.47m (14ft 8in)
Powerplant: One 340kW (450hp) Pratt & Whitney R-985-AN2 Wasp Junior nine-cylinder, air-cooled radial piston engine
Speed: 275km/h (171mph)
Range: 1461km (908 miles)
Ceiling: 5500m (18,200ft)
Crew: 2
Armament: One 7.62mm (0.3in) Browning M1919 machine gun fixed forward-firing in forward fuselage, one 7.62mm (0.3in) Browning M1919 machine gun flexibly mounted in rear cockpit; up to 295kg (650lb) bombload

Supermarine Sea Otter

Intended to replace the Walrus, the service entry of Supermarine's Sea Otter was delayed by several years, although eventually it became the last new biplane design to enter service with both the Royal Navy and RAF.

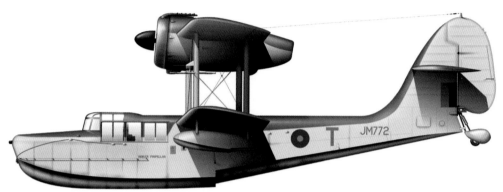

Supermarine Sea Otter Mk.I

Having entered service towards the end of 1944, only four squadrons operated the Sea Otter before the war's end in 1945. One of these units was 292 Squadron, an RAF air sea rescue unit, which operated this aircraft in Ceylon (now Sri Lanka) during 1945.

The maiden flight of the Sea Otter took place on 23 September 1938, prototype construction having been authorized in April 1936. Development had been relatively slow due to Supermarine's other commitments, particularly Spitfire production that was pressing ahead with considerable urgency. Testing revealed a need to alter the propeller from the two-bladed unit originally fitted and alterations to the wings were required to lower the aircraft's landing speed to an acceptable level. With Supermarine possessing no spare production capacity a contract was placed during 1940 with the Blackburn Aircraft Company to produce 190 Sea Otters under licence.

Unfortunately Blackburn too was unable to begin production due to the pressure of other work and the contract was cancelled in 1941. In January 1942, production finally began at Saunders-Roe Ltd, which had already manufactured the Walrus under licence, with the first aircraft off the line taking to the air in January 1943.

Increased load

Despite the lengthy delays, the Sea Otter nonetheless represented a useful increase in capability over the Walrus when it finally entered service in November 1944. With its more powerful Bristol Mercury engine endowing it with a better all-round performance it was capable of carrying a greater load than its predecessor, and thus in the Air Sea Rescue (ASR) role it was able to take off with a higher number of rescued personnel aboard. Unlike the Walrus, the Sea Otter was equipped from the start with an arrestor hook and, although originally intended to undertake gunnery spotting duties, the Sea Otter never served from a catapult-equipped capital ship, all its operational work at sea taking place on carriers. As an ASR machine the Sea Otter proved effective and it continued in service after VJ Day until this mission was taken over by helicopters during the mid-1950s. The Sea Otter also found a useful niche post-war as a versatile

Supermarine Sea Otter

Weight: (Maximum takeoff) 4536kg (10,000lb)
Dimensions: Length: 12.12m (39ft 9in), Wingspan: 14.02m (46ft), Height: 4.93m (16ft 2in)
Powerplant: One 600kW (805hp) Bristol Mercury XXX nine-cylinder air-cooled radial piston engine
Speed: 262km/h (163mph)
Range: 1167km (725 miles)
Ceiling: 5200m (17,000ft)
Crew: 3 or 4
Armament: One 7.7mm (0.303in) Vickers K machine gun flexibly mounted in nose position, two 7.7mm (0.303in) Vickers K machine guns flexibly mounted in dorsal position; up to 440kg (1000lb) bombload

and rugged civilian four-passenger bush aircraft. Of 592 ordered, a total of 292 Sea Otters was built, the remaining 300 being cancelled after the end of hostilities.

Curtiss SO3C Seamew

One of the least satisfactory aircraft of World War II, the SO3C Seamew was plagued with engine and stability problems yet was produced in large numbers and served with both the US and the UK.

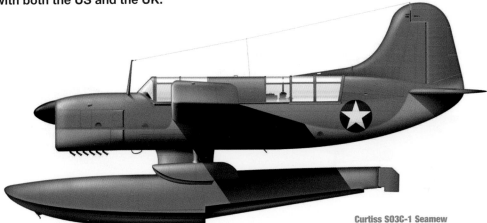

Curtiss SO3C-1 Seamew

Despite its poor general performance, the SO3C did see active service aboard US capital ships. This largely anonymous SO3C-1, Bureau number 4861, was assigned to the light cruiser USS *Denver* but capsized during recovery and was lost on 24 January 1941. Both crewmembers were unhurt.

Intended to replace the successful SOC Seagull, the SO3C originated from a US Navy requirement for a reconnaissance and gunnery spotting aircraft to operate from its cruisers. It was specified that the new aircraft should have better speed and range than the Seagull, possess folding wings and be powered by the Ranger V-770 engine. The prototype Curtiss XSO3C flew on 6 October 1939 and was judged inferior to the competing Vought XO2U-1. Fortunately for Curtiss, Vought had no spare production capacity so the XSO3C was ordered into production instead as the SO3C-1. Oddly, the US Navy initially named it Seagull, causing confusion with its predecessor, the biplane SOC. By the time it entered service, the USN had adopted the British name of Seamew. But all was not well with the new aircraft, as the SO3C was plagued with stability problems that were mitigated, although never eradicated, by enlarging the tail and adding upturned wingtips. More

problematic was the poor reliability of the Ranger V-770 engine that was maintenance heavy and suffered from a tendency to overheat in flight.

First delivery

The first production Seamew was delivered onto the cruiser *Cleveland* on 15 July 1942 and by the end of the year 300 SO3C-1s had been built. Production then switched to the SO3C-2 that featured catapult and arrestor gear for wheeled operation off carriers as well as provision for a single 227kg (500lb) bomb. In total, 456 examples of this variant were produced, with 150 going to the Royal Navy as the Seamew Mk.I.

The final SO3C-3, of which only 44 were built, deleted the catapult gear to save weight and featured a slightly more powerful V-770-8 engine. In US service the Seamew was so unpopular that by early 1944 it was supplanted on catapults by the SOC Seagull it had been designed to replace and

Curtiss SO3C-2 Seamew

Weight: (Maximum takeoff) 2599kg (5729lb)
Dimensions: Length: 11.23m (36ft 10in) on floats, 10.41m (34ft 2in) on wheels, Wingspan: 11.58m (38ft), Height: 4.57m (15ft)
Powerplant: One 450kW (600hp) Ranger V-770-6 inverted V12 air-cooled piston engine
Speed: 277km/h (172mph)
Range: 1850km (1150 miles)
Ceiling: 4800m (15,800ft)
Crew: 2
Armament: One 7.62mm (0.3in) M1919 Browning machine gun fixed forward-firing; one 12.7mm (0.5in) M2 Browning machine gun flexibly mounted in rear cockpit; up to 227kg (500lb) bombload under fuselage (on wheeled version), two 45kg (100lb) bombs or 147kg (325lb) depth charges under wings

relegated to training. In Britain, the final 100 Seamews on order were refused, the Royal Navy receiving Vought OS2U Kingfishers instead.

Sikorsky HNS-1 Hoverfly

Despite being barely operational and available only in trivial numbers, the Sikorsky HNS-1 was the first helicopter available to the Allied navies and paved the way for a revolution in naval aviation.

Although moderately successful, helicopters had already existed for several years, it was Russian émigré Igor Sikorsky who successfully developed the single main rotor with anti-torque tail rotor configuration into a viable aircraft. Sikorsky's VS-300, while strictly an experimental machine, demonstrated the ability to carry underslung loads and operate on both wheels and floats. The developed VS-316 became the XR-4 when accepted by the USAAF in 1942 and exceeded all previous records for helicopter speed, endurance and altitude, and the aircraft was to become the world's first mass-produced helicopter with 131 completed. The USAAF version was designated the R-4, the Navy's were HNS-1s, and it became the Hoverfly Mk.I in British service.

Operational service

A joint committee of US and British representatives was formed to develop the helicopter in operational service. Curiously, the US Navy handed responsibility for introducing the HNS-1 into service use to the Coast Guard. As

such, it was Coast Guard pilot Frank Erikson who flew the first helicopter 'mercy mission' when he used an HNS-1 to ferry blood plasma for injured personnel aboard the destroyer USS *Turner* on 3 January 1944. It was, however, the British who took operational helicopters to sea for the first time. The armed merchant freighter SS *Daghestan* (that had previously been a Sea Hurricane-equipped CAM ship) was fitted with a landing platform at the stern and embarked two float-equipped Hoverfly Is of the Royal Navy. On 6 January 1944 she set sail with convoy HX274 and the Hoverflies flew convoy escort flight trials during the crossing. These proved successful enough that Hoverflies were deployed aboard the escort carrier HMS *Thane* at the end of December. The first US ships with helicopters were six repair vessels that sailed for the South Pacific with two HNS-1s apiece in May 1944. Used to fly spare parts where they were required at short notice, the helicopters were also used for medical evacuation and other mercy missions.

Sikorsky HNS-1

The Sikorsky Hoverfly was difficult to fly, underpowered and limited in capability, but it heralded a new chapter in naval aviation. This example was one of those trialled by the US Coast Guard on behalf of the Navy.

Sikorsky Hoverfly Mk.I

Weight: (Maximum takeoff) 1152kg (2540lb)
Dimensions: Length: 14.66m (48ft 1in) including rotor, Rotor diameter: 11.58m (38ft), Height: 3.78m (12ft 5in)
Powerplant: One 138kW (185hp) Warner R-550-1 seven-cylinder air-cooled radial piston engine
Speed: 121km/h (75mph)
Range: 210km (130 miles)
Ceiling: 2400m (8000ft)
Crew: 2
Armament: None

Curtiss SC Seahawk

Both the final Curtiss design to enter production and the last floatplane intended for use on American capital ships, the SC Seahawk delivered an impressive performance increase over previous aircraft in this class.

Intended to replace both the Vought Kingfisher and Curtiss's own disappointing Seamew, work on what was to become the SC began during 1942 after a request for observation seaplanes was issued by the US Navy. The first of three prototypes flew on 16 February 1944, although 500 production SC-1s had been ordered in June 1943, all of which would be delivered before the end of the war.

Apart from the hugely increased performance, the SC differed most obviously from its predecessors in being a single seater – radar and other navigation aids having improved to the extent that it was no longer seen as necessary to carry a second crew member. The SC was able to be converted from wheels to floats as required, all aircraft being completed as wheeled examples at the factory and flown to Naval Air Stations where the floats, manufactured by Edo under a different contract, were fitted as needed.

Scouting aircraft

Entering service in October 1944, although it didn't see action until June 1945, the primary role of the Seahawk was as a scouting aircraft, but provision was made for the carriage of a stretcher in the fuselage behind the pilot. Often called upon to pick up downed aircrew, the SC-1 was a problematic rescue aircraft as it was difficult to get into the aircraft from the water, pilots took to carrying a knotted line and rope ladder to assist with this procedure. A developed type, the SC-2, featured a jump-seat behind the pilot as well as other improvements but only 10 SC-2s were completed of 450 originally ordered.

The Seahawks persisted on catapult equipped warships in the post-war period as their role was gradually taken over by helicopters, and the last launch of an operational floatplane in USN service occurred in February 1949 from the battleship USS *Missouri*.

Curtiss SC Seahawk

Possessing a similar maximum speed to the F4F Wildcat fighter, the SC Seahawk was a marked improvement in performance terms over its predecessors. This example was assigned to the light cruiser USS *Topeka* when she was commissioned in December 1944.

Curtiss SC-1 Seahawk

Weight: (maximum takeoff) 4082kg (8999lb)

Dimensions: Length: 11.09m (36ft 5in), Wingspan: 12.5m (41ft), Height: 4.88m (16ft)

Powerplant: One 1010kW (1350hp) Wright R-1820-62 Cyclone-cylinder air-cooled radial engine

Speed: 504km/h (313mph)

Range: 1006km (625 miles)

Ceiling: 11,400m (37,300ft)

Crew: 1

Armament: Two 12.7mm (0.5in) M2 Browning machine guns fixed forward firing in wings; up to two 147kg (325lb) bombs under wings

Index

References to illustration captions are in **bold**. References to photographs are in *italics*.

Picture Credits

Photographs:
Air Sea Land Photos: 7, 27, 40, 43, 90, 111
Alamy: 6 (Print Collector), 26 (Historic Image Archiver)
Getty images: 38 (Royal Air Force Museum), 60 (Imperial War Museum), 76 (Royal Air Force Museum), 79 (Print Collector), 91 (Corbis)
Naval History and Heritage Command: 8, 34, 71, 74, 88, 94, 108, 118, 119

Artworks:
Amber Books: 10, 13, 14–15, 17–25, 28–30, 31 top, 32–35, 37, 39, 41, 42, 44, 46, 49 top, 50–53, 54, 57, 62–63, 64 bottom, 65–66, 67 bottom, 68–70, 72–75, 78, 80–87, 89, 92–95, 97–105
David Bocquelet: 45, 55–56, 58, 77, 96, 106–107
Rolando Ugolini: 11–12, 16, 31 bottom, 36, 47–48, 49 bottom, 64 top, 67 top
Teasel Studio: 44, 59, 110–123